Soccer **Skills**

KINGFISHER

a Houghton Mifflin Company imprint
222 Berkeley Street
Boston, Massachusetts 02116
www.houghtonmifflinbooks.com

First published in 2005
2 4 6 8 10 9 7 5 3 1

1TR/0705/TIMS/PICA/128MA/C

Managing editor: Russell Mclean
Coordinating editor: Caitlin Doyle
Designer and picture researcher: Dominic Zwemmer
Illustrators: Mike Buckley, Malcolm Parchment
Picture research manager: Cee Weston-Baker
DTP coordinator: Susanne Olbrich
DTP operator: Primrose Burton
Production controller: Jessamy Oldfield
Indexer: Jennie Morris
U.S. consultant: Bryan Chenault

The publisher would like to thank the following for permission to reproduce their material. Every care has been taken to trace copyright holders. However, if there have been unintentional omissions or failure to trace copyright holders, we apologize and will, if informed, endeavor to make corrections in any future edition.

Cover: Corbis/Dusko Despotovic; pages 3, 7, 13, 17, 21, 25, 27, 29, 30, 33, 35, 39, and 45 Empics/PA; pages 6 and 23 Corbis/Reuters; page 31 Getty Images Sport

Cover image: this image in no way indicates any endorsement or affiliation by David Beckham, his representatives, or any individuals or organizations connected to him.

LIBRARY OF CONGRESS CATALOGING-IN-PUBLICATION DATA
Gifford, Clive.
Soccer skills/Clive Gifford.—1st ed.
p. cm.
Includes index.
1. Soccer—Training—Juvenile literature. I. Title.
GV943.9.T7G54 2005
796.334—dc22   2005006232

ISBN: 0-7534-5932-9
ISBN: 978-07534-5932-4

Printed in China

Soccer **Skills**

Clive Gifford

KINGFISHER

BOSTON

Contents

Getting started

Kickoff   6
Field and players   8
Referees and rules   10

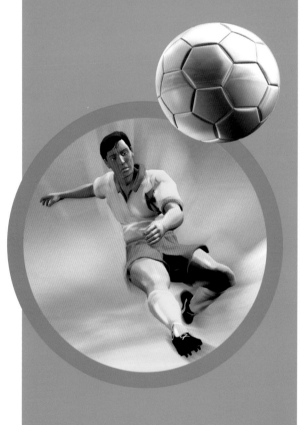

Skills

Ball control   12
Passing   14
Long passing   16
Movement and space   18
Dribbling, shielding,
  and turning   20
Volleying and shooting   22
Heading   24
Tackling   26

Tactics and moves

Tactics   38
Throw-ins and
  corner kicks   40
Free kicks   42
Penalty kicks   44

Position and play

Playing in goal   28
Stunning saves   30
Attacking skills   32
Opening up defenses   34
Defending   36

Reference

Glossary, books,
  and web sites   46
Index   48

Kickoff

Soccer is the world's number one team sport—and there's a good reason for it. It is a thrilling, all-action game, played and watched by millions of people. The best players are worldwide superstars. But everyone can enjoy improving their skills—and helping their side play well.

Ready to play

Always warm up before a game by running, skipping, doing jumping jacks, and jogging with your heels almost touching your bottom. This gets your blood moving around your body. After a warm-up stretch your muscles to help stop injuries. Always hold a stretch for a few seconds and repeat it several times.

▲ Side stretch
This is a side stretch. Stand with your feet apart and reach down to one side as far as you can. Hold the stretch and then repeat it, stretching your other side.

▲ Thigh stretch
This move stretches your thigh muscles. Pull your leg back smoothly and hold the position as you count to ten.

Uniforms

For a soccer game wear a jersey, shorts, and tall soccer socks. Strap shin guards around your lower legs to protect them from kicks. Wear soccer cleats made out of soft leather. They must fit comfortably and support your ankles. You will also need a water bottle and a sweatsuit to keep you warm when you are not playing.

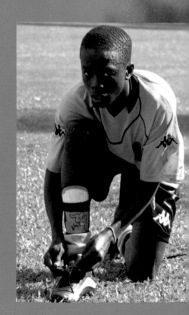

◀ **Superstar forward**
Ukrainian forward Andriy
Shevchenko plays in Italy for
AC Milan. Here, he jumps to
bring the ball under control.
You can read more about
ball control on pages 12–13.

Top tips

- Always keep your
  uniform and cleats
  in good condition.
- If your cleats have
  screw-in studs, check
  that each stud is
  tight before a game.
- When you are
  training or playing,
  take small drinks
  of water often.

Field and players

The field is where everything happens. For a full game the field measures around 110 yards long and 75 yards wide. Each side has 11 players that usually line up in groups of defenders, midfielders, and attackers (see page 38). They play two half games of 45 minutes each, plus any time for injuries or other breaks in the game. During the game the coach or manager of a team can replace one or more players with substitutes.

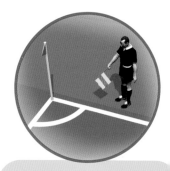

▲ Corner kick
A goal kick or a corner kick is given when the ball goes over the goal line. Here, the referee's assistant signals for a corner kick

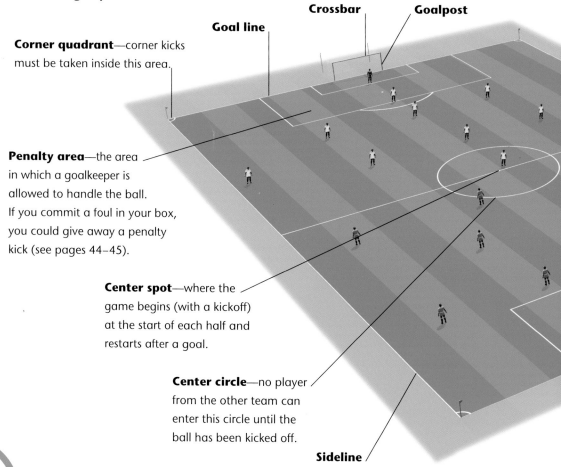

Crossbar

Goalpost

Goal line

Corner quadrant—corner kicks must be taken inside this area.

Penalty area—the area in which a goalkeeper is allowed to handle the ball. If you commit a foul in your box, you could give away a penalty kick (see pages 44–45).

Center spot—where the game begins (with a kickoff) at the start of each half and restarts after a goal.

Center circle—no player from the other team can enter this circle until the ball has been kicked off.

Sideline

Ball in play   **Ball out of play**

n or out of play?

/hen the ball is on the field, it is said to
e in play. When it leaves the field, it is
ut of play. For a ball to be out of play
e entire ball has to cross the line.

Goal

No goal

No goal

No goal

Goal or no goal?

For a goal to be allowed by the referee,
the entire ball must cross the line between
the goalposts. Here, only the ball at the
very top is a goal.

Halfway line—divides the field into
two equal-sized areas of play. Players have
to stay in their own half before a kickoff.

Penalty spot—the area
from where penalty kicks
are taken.

▶ Throw-in

When the ball goes out
of play on the sidelines, the
referee's assistant signals for a
throw-in. He or she points the
flag toward the goal that the
throwing-in team is attacking.

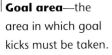

Goal area—the
area in which goal
kicks must be taken.

Referees and rules

The referee and the assistants run the game. They judge whether the ball has gone out of play and which team touched it last. The referee blows a whistle to stop the game if a player is caught offside or commits a foul. Fouls include handball, pushing, tripping or kicking an opponent, shirt-pulling, and bad language. Referees award free kicks or penalty kicks if a serious foul happens inside the penalty area.

Advantage

If you are fouled while you are in a good position, the referee can choose to let the game continue instead of giving a free kick. It is called "playing advantage." Above is the referee's signal for it.

Yellow and red

A yellow card is a warning. If you get two yellow cards in one game or commit a very serious offense, such as a dangerous foul, you are shown a red card. You have to leave the field and are out of the game. Your team must continue with one player less.

▲ Foul
This player has committed a deliberate and dangerous foul to stop a forward who has a clear chance of scoring. The referee often shows a red card for this type of foul.

Offside

When a teammate passes the ball forward, two opposing players must be either level with you or between you and the opponent's goal. If not, the referee may blow for offside and give the other team a free kick. The offside rule does not count if:

- you are behind the ball when it is kicked;
- you receive the ball directly from a throw-in, a corner kick, or a goal kick;
- you are in your own half of the field;
- in the referee's opinion, you are not involved in play or gaining an advantage.

Signal for offside

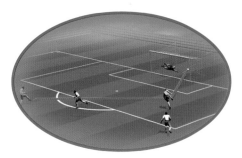

▲ Offside
The goal scorer is offside when the ball is played to him. The goal is not given, and the other team gets a free kick.

▲ Not offside
The scorer is in front of the goalkeeper, but there are two defenders between him and the goal. He is not offside.

Not involved
The player in yellow and red (just inside the penalty area) is not involved in play when his teammate shoots. The referee awards the goal.

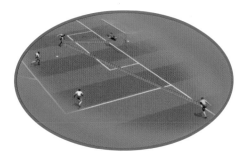

▲ Not offside
You are not offside if you are behind the ball when it is played. Here, the scorer is not offside, and the goal is allowed by the referee.

11

Ball control

A soccer ball can zip around the field at great speeds. Cushioning helps you get the ball under control. Keep your body relaxed and balanced. As the ball arrives, move the part of your body that will make contact with the ball back or down in the direction in which the ball is moving. This slows the ball down and keeps it from bouncing away.

Ball trapping

Trapping is a way to control a rolling ball. Use the sole of your cleat to firmly hold the ball in place. Do not stamp on the ball, or it might pop out from under your foot.

Sidefoot cushion

1 A sidefoot cushion is a good way to control a ball that is skidding across the field. Move your weight onto your standing foot, using your arms for balance.

2 As the ball arrives, lift your leg and try to bring the ball down with the side of your foot.

Thigh cushion

You can cushion a high, falling ball with your thigh. Raise your upper leg so that it is almost parallel to the ground. As the ball arrives, move your leg down to cushion it. Try to drop the ball in front of your feet.

3 The ball should drop to the ground, ready for you to make a pass to another player. You could also run with the ball or take a shot.

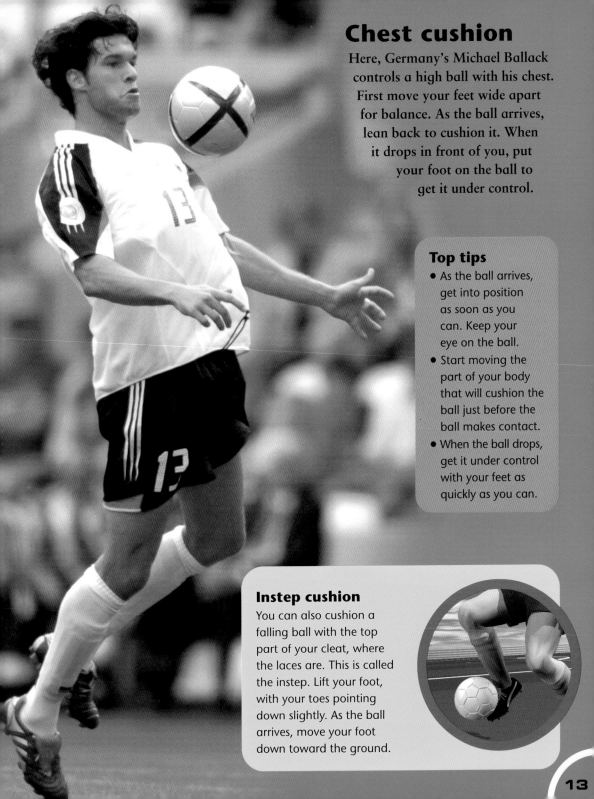

Chest cushion

Here, Germany's Michael Ballack controls a high ball with his chest. First move your feet wide apart for balance. As the ball arrives, lean back to cushion it. When it drops in front of you, put your foot on the ball to get it under control.

Top tips

- As the ball arrives, get into position as soon as you can. Keep your eye on the ball.
- Start moving the part of your body that will cushion the ball just before the ball makes contact.
- When the ball drops, get it under control with your feet as quickly as you can.

Instep cushion

You can also cushion a falling ball with the top part of your cleat, where the laces are. This is called the instep. Lift your foot, with your toes pointing down slightly. As the ball arrives, move your foot down toward the ground.

Passing

Passing is the most important skill to master in soccer. It connects players all over the field and allows a team to build attacks. Practice your passing as often as you can by copying the top players. Work even harder with your weaker foot. A player who can pass well with both fe can often win the game!

idefoot pass

ɔu can use the
side of your foot
make a sidefoot
push pass. This
the simplest pass,
d it is the easiest to
ntrol because more of
ur foot touches the ball
an with any other pass.
is used to hit the ball
ort or medium distances
d for close shots that
e close to the goal.

1 Position your body over the ball with your standing foot beside it.

2 Swing your leg and push through the middle of the ball with the inside of your foot.

3 Follow through smoothly, keeping your eye on the ball as you pass.

ircle passing

etting your passes to the target is crucial. Try this fun
ɪssing drill, with four players standing around the edge
the center circle and another player in the middle. The
iddle player receives a pass. Then he or she turns and hits
ɪ accurate sidefoot pass so that the person who gets the
ɪll does not have to move to control it.

◀ Pressure pass

Under pressure from an
opponent this player has
made a good sidefoot pass.
His foot has followed through
and is pointing in the direction
in which the ball is traveling.

Long passing

The instep pass is the most common pass for hitting the ball longer distances. You can use it for shots too. Position your body over the ball, with your nonkicking foot next to it. Point your toes downward and aim to hit the middle of the ball with the laces of your cleat. Keep your foot stretched and your toes pointing downward as you swing your leg smoothly through to the ball. Your foot should end up pointing in the direction of the pass.

▶ **Pass star**
The U.S.'s Brandi Chastain hits a long instep pass while on the move. Vary how far a pass travels by taking a longer or shorter swing of your leg and by moving your kicking leg faster or slower.

Lofted instep drive

This is similar to an instep pass, but it sends the ball higher and farther. Use it for passes and to make clearances out of defense.

1 Your standing foot should be placed to the side and slightly behind the ball. Swing your kicking leg smoothly, with your toes pointing downward.

2 Aim to hit the bottom half of the ball. Lean back slightly, as this helps send the ball higher. Keep your eye on the ball.

3 After hitting the ball, your foot should foll• through and move across yo body slightly. Practice hittin• this pass with different amounts of force.

Three against one

To practice instep and sidefoot passing while under pressure, mark out a small area with four cones. A team of three players has to pass the ball without a fourth player getting it. When the ball leaves the area or the fourth player gets the ball, he or she switches with one of the team of three.

Top tips

- Check your target just before you make a pass.
- Try to hit the ball smoothly and with the right amount of force.
- Use the sidefoot pass for shorter passing. Use the instep drive for longer passing.
- Work on all types of passes with both feet. Practice passing and receiving the ball with your friends.

Movement and space

Once you have made a pass, don't stand there and admire it—start moving! You should be looking for space on the field in which you can receive a pass from a teammate. Quick, accurate passing and moving between two or more players can open up a game and quickly move the ball across the field.

Player 1

▶ One-two pass

A simple but very useful passing move is the one-two pass, or wall pass. Here, Player 1 passes to a teammate. He then sprints past the opponent in red and receives a quick return pass ahead of him. The pass cuts out the defender.

Triangle passing

Practice your passing and moving using the game on page 17, as well as with this triangles drill. With two teammates, pass and move your way up and down a field. When you get the ball, make a short, accurate pass. Then sprint into an open space to receive the ball again.

Passing and moving

Soccer is a game that changes fast. A great, op position to receive a pass in could be blocked i instant. So when you are looking to receive a p be alert and ready to move. Making quick pas while moving is a tricky skill. Usually you can aim where the player is, but instead at where you think he or she will be when the ball arrive You need to judge how fast your teammate is moving and how far away he or she is.

Player 1

Decoy run

A decoy is when a player moves as if he or she wants to receive the ball but is, in fact, trying to make space for a teammate. At this throw-in Player 1 has moved toward the thrower, and a defender has followed him. This has created space farther up the field for a teammate to run into and receive the throw.

Five-a-side

Play a five-a-side game to practice your passing and moving skills. Here, a player beats an opponent by using the wall of the field to make a one-two pass to himself.

1 The attacker is blocked in by two defenders.

2 He plays the ball against the wall . . .

3 . . . and collects the rebound.

Dribbling, shielding, and turning

When you run with the ball and try to beat defenders, it is called dribbling. Keep the ball close to you and under control at all times. As you move, tap the ball forward with the inside and outside of your feet. In order to beat opponents you will also need to be able to shield the ball, turn, and fake.

Faking

Faking is pretending to turn one way to fool an opponent before turning a different way.

1 The dribbling player (in red) fakes to turn right. He leans to the right and drops his right shoulder.

2 The defender lunges to the attacker's right.

3 The dribbler fools the defender by turning to the left and dribbling past him.

Shielding

1 Shielding is a way of keeping the ball when you are under pressure. This player has received a pass just as an opponent quickly closes in.

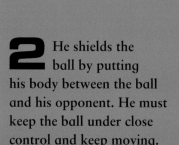

2 He shields the ball by putting his body between the ball and his opponent. He must keep the ball under close control and keep moving.

3 While shielding the ball, he must not push or foul his opponent. He looks for his next move and makes a sidefoot pass to a teammate.

◄ **Star dribbler**
Manchester United's
Wayne Rooney dribbles
through a packed defense.
He is balanced and has
his eye on the ball as
he makes a sharp turn.

Outside hook

One way to turn with the
ball is to use an outside
hook. Lean in the direction
that you want to turn and
hook the outside of your foot
around the ball. Swivel on your
standing foot and drag the ball
around with you as you turn.

21

Volleying and shooting

When you shoot, there is no point kicking the ball really hard if your shot is not aimed at the target. If you are close to the goal, you can shoot with a strong sidefoot pass (see page 15). From farther away try an instep pass (see page 16).

Volley

Kicking the ball when it is up in the air is called a volley. Use it to move the ball a long distance or to hit a powerful shot.

1 To hit a front-on volley lift your knee as the ball gets close. Then swing your leg with your toes pointing downward.

2 Make contact with the ball on the laces of your cleat. Remember to keep your head over the ball.

Half volley

A half volley is when the ball is kicked right after it has hit the ground. Stretch your ankle so that your toes point at the ground. Keep your body over the ball so that it stays down after you have kicked it.

▶ Side volley
Michael Owen hits a powerful side volley for his team, Real Madrid. His leg is parallel to the ground, and he is closely watching the ball.

Shoot

Practice your shooting by using chalk to mark out four squares on a wall. Ask a friend to pass the ball to you and then aim for a different square each time you kick the ball.

Heading

Heading does not hurt when you use the correct technique. If you are nervous about heading, practice with a soft ball in order to build up your skills. Start with headers from a standing position, with one foot behind the other and your knees bent. This gives you a stable base.

1 As the ball travels through the air, pull back your upper body and head a little. Remember to keep your eyes open.

2 Push your head forward to meet the ball with the middle of your forehead. Keep your neck muscles firm in order to help push the ball away.

Heading down

For most headers you will be trying to get slightly over the ball in order to direct it downward to a teammate's feet or toward the goal. Practice downward headers with this heading drill. After five headers in a row swap positions with your partner.

1 One player gently throws the ball to his or her partner with an underhand throw.

2 The other player heads the ball down to the feet of the thrower.

Defensive header

Defenders often have to direct powerful headers up and out of the way of their penalty area. When you are clearing the ball away from danger, head the ball at the top of your jump. Try to get a lot of distance and height to your header.

Heading goals

Many goals are scored by headers, especially from corner kicks or passes into the goal area. This attacker has jumped up high to get his head above the ball. He guides it down into the corner of the goal, leaving the goalkeeper with no chance.

▶ Power header

For maximum distance and force you need to make a power header. Here, the Republic of Ireland's Robbie Keane springs forward to meet the ball in midair. He thrusts his arms backward to help drive his neck and head forward to meet the ball.

Tackling

All players have to tackle—not just defenders. Tackles
work best when you have teammates nearby to cover you,
but sometimes you have no choice except to make a tackle to
stop the chance of a goal. Tackling requires perfect timing. Once
you decide to make a tackle, go for it directly and keep your eye
on the ball. Try to stay on your feet. This allows you to pass the
ball if you get it or chase back if your tackle is unsuccessful.

Front block tackle

The most common tackles are called block tackles
because you use your foot to block the path of the
ball and force it away from your opponent.

1 The player
in white bends
his knees, ready to
make the tackle.

2 He uses
the inside
of his foot to make
contact with the
middle of the ball.

3 If the ball gets
stuck, he tries
to roll the ball over
or flick it away from
the opponent's foot.

4 When the
ball is free,
he moves away
to get the ball
under control.

Clearing the ball
Sometimes winning a tackle in your penalty
area gives you enough time to choose who
to pass the ball to. At other times you may
be under pressure immediately. This is when
you should hit a long, quick clearance.

◄ Perfect timing

Brazilian defender Cafu (in white) moves in to kick the ball away from winger Cristiano Ronaldo during a Champions League game. To make tackles and interceptions you have to time your challenge well.

Playing in goal

Goalkeepers are the only players on the field who are allowed to handle the ball—but only inside of their own penalty area. A lot of the time a goalkeeper can keep the goal safe by staying alert and giving intructions to his or her defenders. When the other team attacks, the goalkeeper should stand on the balls of his or her feet with legs apart and knees bent. This allows the goalkeeper to move quickly—to run out to meet the ball with a kick or a catch or to dive to one side and make a save.

Narrowing the angle

1 An attacker has the ball and is running toward the goal. The goalkeeper reacts by moving from the goal line and toward the attacker. He is narrowing the angle.

2 The goalkeeper stays upright as he closes in on the attacker. He tries to block as much of the goal as possible from the attacker's view. This makes it harder to score.

- Get your body behind a ball that you are trying to stop or catch.
- Watch the ball until it is in your hands.
- Pay attention to the game and talk to your teammates.
- If you decide to go for a ball in a crowded penalty area, call out loudly and go for it.

Gathering the ball

To collect a low ball drop down into one knee and lean forward with your body in line with the ball's direction. Gather the ball and scoop it up close to your body to keep it safe.

3 The goalkeeper dives for the ball at the feet of an attacker. He stretches himself and gets his hands on the ball to quickly gather it into his body.

▶ **Safe catch**
German goalkeeper Oliver Kahn makes a catch above his head. To hold the ball safely his hands are behind the ball on each.

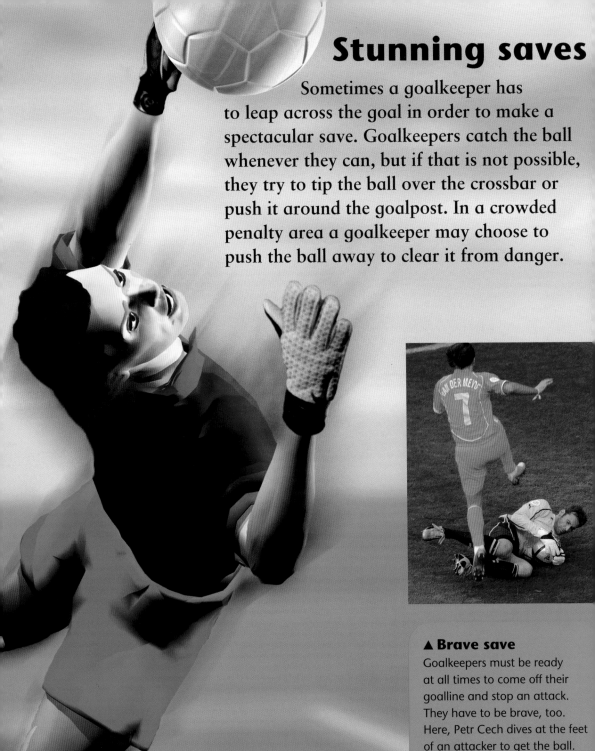

Stunning saves

Sometimes a goalkeeper has to leap across the goal in order to make a spectacular save. Goalkeepers catch the ball whenever they can, but if that is not possible, they try to tip the ball over the crossbar or push it around the goalpost. In a crowded penalty area a goalkeeper may choose to push the ball away to clear it from danger.

▲ **Brave save**
Goalkeepers must be ready at all times to come off their goalline and stop an attack. They have to be brave, too. Here, Petr Cech dives at the feet of an attacker to get the ball.

Making a diving save

1 Standing on the balls of his feet, the goalkeeper starts to move across the goal.

2 He pushes off from one foot to start diving to his left. He tries to keep his eyes on the ball.

3 He stretches his arms out and gets his hands behind the ball with his fingers spread out.

4 He gathers the ball into his chest and protects it from falling out of his hands as he lands.

Releasing the ball

After making a save a goalkeeper has six seconds to release the ball. A long kick up the field or a quick throw to a teammate in a clear area can help start an attack. Goalkeepers have to be able to kick a rolling ball well because of the backpass rule. When a teammate uses his or her feet to pass the ball back to the goalkeeper, he or she cannot pick it up. Instead the goalkeeper must head the ball or kick it clear.

◄ Underhand throw

Norway's Bente Nordby has spotted a teammate with lots of space and is rolling the ball out underhand. After releasing the ball, her arm will follow through to point at her target.

Attacking skills

Teams can attack in many different ways. They can quickly turn from defense into attack by gaining the ball and kicking a long pass to a striker who has remained farther up the field. They can cross the ball into the penalty area or chip the ball over opponents into an open space. They can also patiently build up an attack by using many short passes.

Crosses

A cross is a pass from wide out into the penalty area. Look up to see where your teammates are and then hit the ball with plenty of pace, or speed. This attacker has used a lofted instep drive (see page 16) to hit a high cross, aiming for the head of a teammate close to the goal.

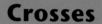

Chipping

A chip is a pass or a shot that rises high up into the air. You can use it to move the ball over the head of a defender in order to get it to a teammate who is in an open space. A chip can also beat a goalkeeper who is a long way away from the goal line.

1 To hit a chip you need to strike the bottom of the ball.

2 Use a strong downward thrust of your foot to make contact.

3 Keep your follow-through short. The ball should rise steeply up into the air.

Push and go

In some attacking situations you can beat a defender not by dribbling but by making a pass to yourself. This is called a push and go. Carefully push a pass beyond the defender. As soon as the ball leaves your foot, sprint quickly to collect the ball.

▼ Quick control

Arsenal's Thierry Henry (in yellow) uses his great pace to push the ball ahead and sprint past a defender. He has moved the ball ahead of him a short distance, but not too far that he cannot quickly regain control of it again.

Opening up defenses

It can often get crowded in and around the penalty area that you are attacking. Space can be hard to find, and you may be closely guarded, or marked, by an opposing player. When you are running toward the goal, make a sudden change of direction and move away from your marker and into an open space for a pass. One helpful tip is to lean and take a step in one direction. Then swivel on one foot and sprint away in a different direction.

Player 1   Player 2

Making space

You can create space for a teammate to attack by running in one direction, which causes your marker to move with you. Here, Player 1 has sprinted to the left. This has left a gap, which Player 2 will run into to receive a pass.

Overlap

You can use the full width of the field to create extra space for an attack. An attacker who runs down the sideline ahead of the ball creates an overlap.

1 The attacker is close to the edge of the field. As he gets close to the defender in red, he passes the ball to a teammate.

2 The defender cannot make up his mind. This allows the attacker a chance to run down the line.

3 The attacker receives a return pass. He may be able to hit a cross or run with the ball toward the goal

Back heel

Sometimes a back heel in a crowded penalty area can fool opponents and give a teammate the chance to take a shot. Strike through the middle of the ball with your heel or the sole of your cleat.

- A good way to create openings for attack is to quickly pass the ball between players using as few touches as possible. Practice one- and two-touch passing moves with your friends.
- If your team has a shot at making a goal, follow the ball in. Be alert in case it rebounds toward you.
- Do not be afraid to tave a shot if you are in the penalty area and you cannot see a better option.

hrough balls

rough passes are attacking passes that travel hind opposing defenders. Here, Player 1 has 1yed the ball ahead of Player 2 (the receiver) that he can run into the ball. A through ss has to be hit with the right amount of rce for the receiver to be able to reach it.

ayer 2

Player 1

Defending

Defending may not be as exciting as attacking and scoring goals, but it is just as important. When your team loses control of the ball, the entire side must defend in order to stop the opposing team from scoring and to win the ball back. Try to get in between the ball and your goal, filling up space that the other side may want to attack in. You should guard and cover opponents as they make attacking runs.

Interception

All players must work hard in order to win the ball back for their side. This alert forward (in blue) has spotted a weak pass and intercepted the ball.

◀ Two against one

Two Sparta Prague defenders work together to challenge Lyon's Sydney Govou. One defender keeps guarding while his teammate (on the right) prepares to make a tackle.

▲ Slowing down

A defender (in blue shorts) is jockeying an attacker who has his back toward the goal. This gives his side enough time to get into a good defensive position.

Jockeying

Delaying the player who has the ball is called jockeying. Close in on the opponent until you are four to six feet away. Stand on the balls of your feet, with your knees bent and your arms out for balance. Try to stay between your goal and the other player, slowing him or her down. If a teammate arrives to cover you, try to make a tackle to gain the ball.

Top tips

- Talk to your teammates and defend together.
- Do not dive into a tackle unless teammates are behind you as cover.
- Jockey an opponent who has the ball to slow him or her down as much as possible.
- If you are guarding a player one-on-one, stay with him or her at all times. Do not get distracted.
- When you clear the ball out of defense, do it quickly and safely.

Marking

The defender in blue is guarding an attacker one-on-one. He stays close to the attacker, giving him less time and space to get to the ball. One-on-one markers try to stay between the player they are guarding and their own goal.

Tactics

Tactics are the way in which a team chooses to play a game—as well as its plans for winning. Tactics can involve using special moves—such as corner kicks and free kicks, which can be practiced in training—or marking an especially dangerous opponent throughout the game. Coaches can change tactics during a game, depending on how it is going.

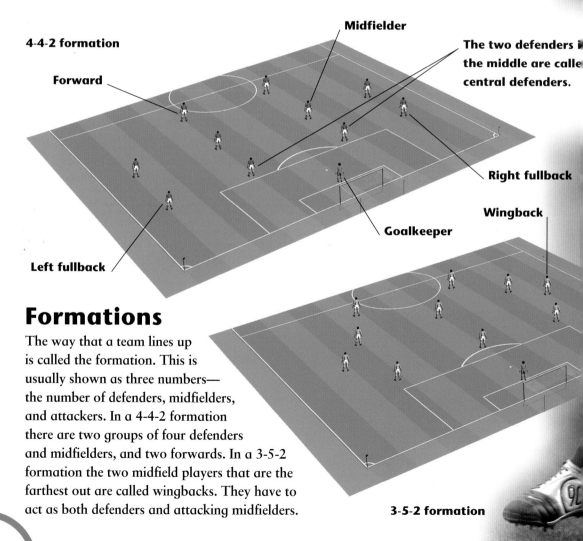

4-4-2 formation

Midfielder

Forward

The two defenders in the middle are called central defenders.

Right fullback

Wingback

Goalkeeper

Left fullback

Formations

The way that a team lines up is called the formation. This is usually shown as three numbers— the number of defenders, midfielders, and attackers. In a 4-4-2 formation there are two groups of four defenders and midfielders, and two forwards. In a 3-5-2 formation the two midfield players that are the farthest out are called wingbacks. They have to act as both defenders and attacking midfielders.

3-5-2 formation

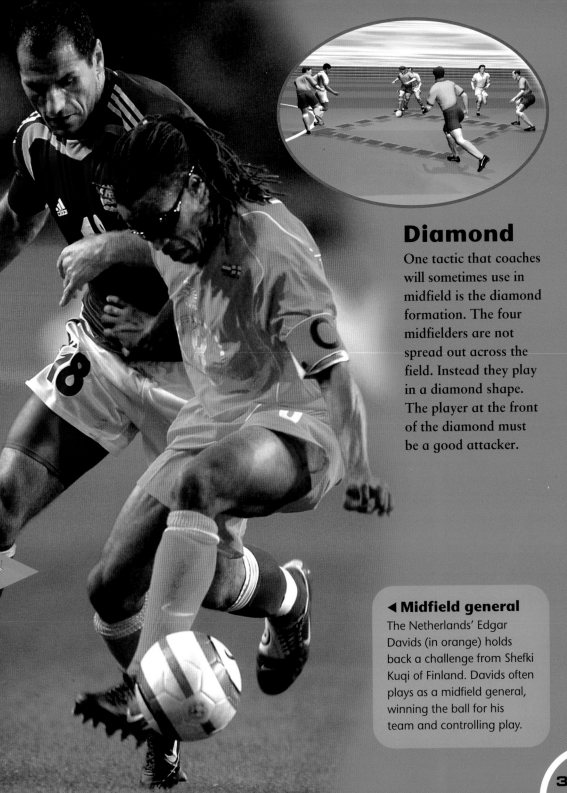

Diamond

One tactic that coaches will sometimes use in midfield is the diamond formation. The four midfielders are not spread out across the field. Instead they play in a diamond shape. The player at the front of the diamond must be a good attacker.

◀ **Midfield general**

The Netherlands' Edgar Davids (in orange) holds back a challenge from Shefki Kuqi of Finland. Davids often plays as a midfield general, winning the ball for his team and controlling play.

Throw-ins and corner kicks

When the ball goes out of play, the referee will signal for a throw-in, a corner kick, or a goal kick. A throw-in is awarded when the ball goes over the sideline. When you take a throw-i both feet must be on the ground behind the side and both hands must be on the ball. Corner kick are given if the ball crosses the goal line and the defending team touched it last.

◄ Throw-in grip
Spread your hands around the back and sides of the ball so that your thumbs almost touch. This gives you a good grip on the ball.

Throw-in

To take a throw-in bring the ball back behind your head and then bend your back and bring your hands forward. Let go of the ball just before your arms come over your head.

► Return pass
Once you have taken a throw-in, step back onto the field in case the player who receives the throw passes the ball right back to you.

Corner kicks

This player is aiming to hit a corner kick into the goal area. When you strike a corner kick, make sure that you are well balanced on your standing leg and hit through the middle of the ball. Your kicking leg should follow through and across your body.

Top tips

- When you take a corner kick, aim for a target just above head height.
- Make sure you are completely balanced on your nonkicking foot.
- Strike the ball hard enough to carry it into the six-yard box.
- Surprise your opponents by occasionally hitting a short corner kick.

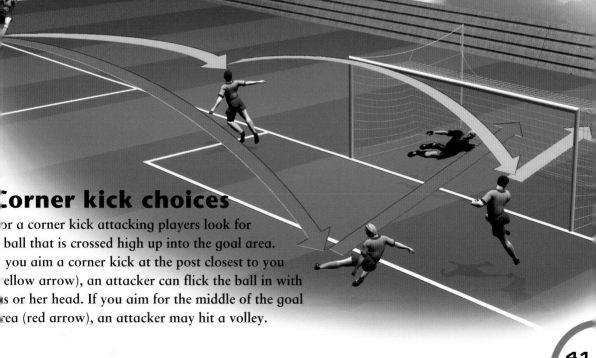

Corner kick choices

or a corner kick attacking players look for
ball that is crossed high up into the goal area.
you aim a corner kick at the post closest to you
ellow arrow), an attacker can flick the ball in with
s or her head. If you aim for the middle of the goal
ea (red arrow), an attacker may hit a volley.

Free kicks

When a referee blows the whistle for offside, a dangerous tackle, or another type of foul, he or she will usually award a free kick to one team. The ball is placed on the ground, and the opposing side must move back ten yards. There are two types of free kicks.

Signal for an indirect free kick

Signal for a direct free kick

◄ Direct or indirect
You can score directly from a direct free kick. With an indirect free kick, you must pass the ball to a teammate.

Attacking free kicks

Free kicks in front of and close to the other team's goal allow your team the chance to score. Defending teams will often set up a wall of their players to block a direct shot into the goal. You have to find a way around that wall.

Skillful players try to bend or swerve the ball around or over the wall

Defensive wall

A pass to this player may give him a clear shot at the goal.

Top tips

- When you take a free kick in the middle of the field, a short, quick pass can often release a teammate.
- Do not try to blast a shot from a free kick into the goal when you are a long way away from the goal. Instead, make a pass or cross the ball into the penalty area.
- Vary your free kicks throughout a game. This keeps the other team guessing.

Bending the ball

To hit an outside swerve kick through the side of the ball with the outside of your foot. As you follow through your foot should move across your body. To hit an inside swerve kick low through the side of the ball with the inside of your foot. Your follow-through should be straight.

Outside swerve

Penalty kicks

If there is a deliberate hand ball or a serious foul in the penalty area, the referee will award a free shot at the goal. This is called a penalty kick. Only the penalty kick taker and the goalkeeper are allowed in the penalty area during the tense moments leading up to the penalty kick. But teammates stand around the edge of the area, ready to race in if the shot rebounds off the goalkeeper, the goalposts, or the crossbar.

Taking a penalty kick

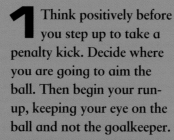

1 Think positively before you step up to take a penalty kick. Decide where you are going to aim the ball. Then begin your run-up, keeping your eye on the ball and not the goalkeeper.

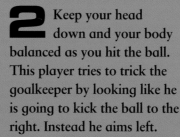

2 Keep your head down and your body balanced as you hit the ball. This player tries to trick the goalkeeper by looking like he is going to kick the ball to the right. Instead he aims left.

3 The penalty kick taker hits a firm sidefoot pass low into the corner of the goal. He has beaten the goalkeeper, who dived the wrong way. He scores!

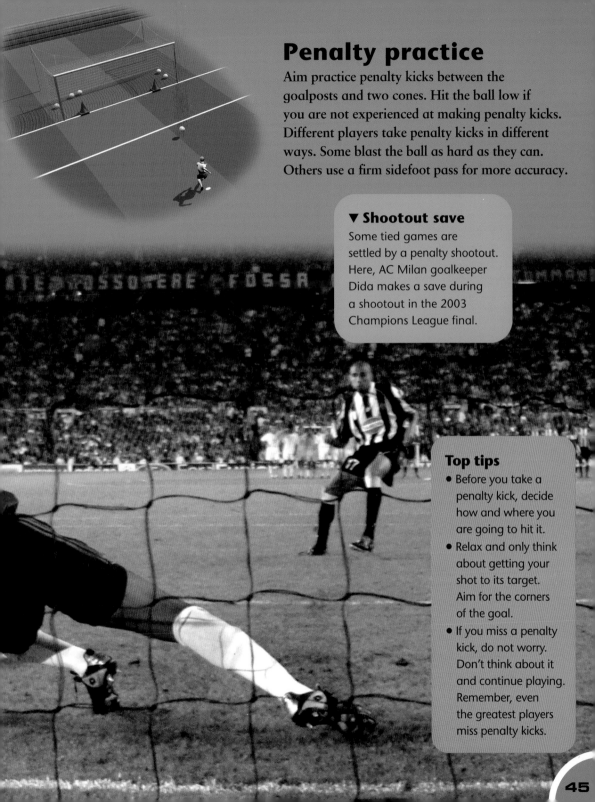

Penalty practice

Aim practice penalty kicks between the goalposts and two cones. Hit the ball low if you are not experienced at making penalty kicks. Different players take penalty kicks in different ways. Some blast the ball as hard as they can. Others use a firm sidefoot pass for more accuracy.

▼ Shootout save

Some tied games are settled by a penalty shootout. Here, AC Milan goalkeeper Dida makes a save during a shootout in the 2003 Champions League final.

Top tips

- Before you take a penalty kick, decide how and where you are going to hit it.
- Relax and only think about getting your shot to its target. Aim for the corners of the goal.
- If you miss a penalty kick, do not worry. Don't think about it and continue playing. Remember, even the greatest players miss penalty kicks.

Glossary

advantage When the referee does not stop the game for a foul because the team that was fouled against benefits from the game continuing.

booking An official warning given to a player by the referee.

box Another name for the penalty area.

chip A pass that is hit steeply into the air from one player to a teammate or as a shot at the goal.

clearance A kick or header of the ball out of defense.

cross A kick of the ball from the sideline to the center of the field, usually into the other team's penalty area.

cushion To slow a ball down (in order to control it) by using a part of the body.

direct free kick A kick awarded to a team. A goal can be scored directly from this type of free kick.

dribble To move the ball under tight control with a series of short kicks or taps.

fake To pretend to move one way to trick an opponent.

formation The way in which a team's players line up on the field.

foul A player commits a foul when he or she breaks one of the rules of soccer.

goal kick A kick taken from the goal area after the ball has rolled over the goal line.

halftime A break, usually 15 minutes long, between the two halves of a game.

hand ball A type of foul that occurs when a player touches the ball with his or her hands or arms.

indirect free kick A kick given to a team from which a goal cannot be scored directly.

instep The top of a soccer cleat, where the laces are.

jockey To delay an opponent who has the ball.

kickoff The move from the center spot that starts the game after a goal or at the start of each half.

narrowing the angle When a goalkeeper moves toward an attacker so that the attacker can see less of the goal and has a smaller target to aim at.

one-on-one mark To guard an opponent in order to stop him or her from getting the ball.

one-two pass A pair of passes between two players that send the ball past a defender. It is also known as a wall pass.

pace Speed.

penalty shootout A way to settle a tied game in some competitions. Five players per side take one penalty shot each. If the scores are even after ten penalty kicks, other players take penalty kicks until one player misses.

referee's assistant An official who helps the referee run a game. Assistants used to be known as linesmen.

elding Placing your
dy between the ball
d an opposing player
protect the ball.

kle To take the ball
ay from an opponent
ng your feet.

tics Ways of playing
ame used to outwit and
at the opposing team.

ough pass An attacking
ss that is played behind
lefender to a teammate.

row-in
rowing the
ll back into play
ter it has crossed
e sideline. The
ll must be thrown
om the place where
crossed the line.

lley A kick made at the
ll when it is off the ground.

all A line of defenders
anding close together to
otect their goal against
free kick.

Books

*The Kingfisher Soccer
Encyclopedia* by Clive
Gifford, Kingfisher

A superb soccer reference
book, including profiles
of the world's greatest
players, teams, coaches,
and competitions.

*Kids' Book of Soccer: Skills,
Strategies, Equipment, and
the Rules of the Game* by
Brooks Clark, Citadel Press

A clear guide to the basics
of playing the game and
the laws of soccer.

Soccer by Clive Gifford,
Kingfisher

The award-winning book
of skills, tactics, soccer
stars, and great games.

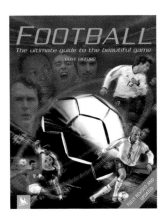

Web sites

**www.clivegifford.co.uk/
inprint/football.htm**
The home of the author's
Web pages dedicated to
soccer. Includes Web links
to other soccer sites, funny
quotes, training tips,
and notes on skills.

**www.joesoccer.com/info/
games.html**
View a selection of
animated games and drills
to improve your skills.

www.fa-soccerstar.com
Home of the Soccer
Star coaching program.
It contains videos, cartoons,
and training tips about key
skills such as dribbling
and shooting.

**www.soccerlinks.net/
index.html**
A huge collection of Web
links to soccer web sites. Find
out anything and everything
you can about soccer.

Index

advantage 10, 11, 46
attacking 32–35

back heels 35
backpass rule 31
Ballack, Michael 13

Cafu 27
cards 10
Cech, Petr 30
Chastain, Brandi
  17
chipping 32, 46
clearing 16, 22,
  25, 26, 46
cleats 6, 7
corner kicks 8, 25, 38, 40, 41
crossing 16, 25, 32, 43, 46
cushioning 12–13
  chest cushioning 13
  instep cushioning 13
  sidefoot cushioning 12
  thigh cushioning 12

Davids, Edgar 39
decoy runs 19
defending 25, 28, 36–37
Dida 45
dribbling 20, 21, 33, 46
driving the ball 16, 17, 32

faking 20, 46
fields 8–9
five-a-side games 19
formations 38–39

fouls 8, 10, 42, 44
free kicks 10, 38, 42–43, 46

goal kicks 8, 9, 11, 31, 40, 46
goalkeepers 28–31, 32, 44
Govou, Sydney 36

heading 24–25
Henry, Thierry 33

interceptions 37

jockeying 37, 46

Kahn, Oliver 29
Keane, Robbie 25

marking 36

Nordby, Bente 29

offside rule 11
one-touch play 35
outside hooks 21
overlaps 34
Owen, Michael 22

passing 12, 14–17, 18, 19,
  22, 32, 33, 34, 35, 40, 43, 44
  instep passing 14, 16, 17
  one-two passing 18, 19, 46
  outside passing 14
  push and go passing 33
  sidefoot passing 14,
    15, 17, 22, 44
  triangle passing 18
penalty kicks 8, 9, 10,
  44–45

penalty shootouts 45, 46

referees 10–11
Ronaldo, Cristiano 27
Rooney, Wayne 21
rules 10–11

saves 28, 29, 30–31
Shevchenko, Andriy 7
shielding 20, 47
shooting 15, 16, 22, 23,
  42–43, 44, 45
stretching 6
swerving the ball 42, 43

tackling 26–27, 36, 37, 42,
  block tackling 26
tactics 38–39, 47
through passes 35, 47
throw-ins 9, 11, 31, 40, 47
trapping 12
triangle passes 18

uniforms 6, 7

volleying 22, 41, 47

warming up 6
wingbacks 38

The Battle of Belleau Wood

Books in the Battles Series:

The Battle of Belleau Wood

The Battle of Britain

The Battle of Gettysburg

The Battle of Hastings

The Battle of Marathon

The Battle of Midway

The Battle of Waterloo

The Battle of Zama

The Inchon Invasion

The Invasion of Normandy

☆ Battles of World War I ☆

The Battle of Belleau Wood

by Earle Rice Jr.

Lucent Books, P.O. Box 289011, San Diego, CA 92198-9011

Library of Congress Cataloging-in-Publication Data

Rice, Earle
    The Battle of Belleau Wood / Earle Rice Jr.
      p. cm. — (Battles of World War I)
    Includes bibliographical references and index.
    Summary: Describes the events before, during, and after the Battle
of Belleau Wood in World War I.
    ISBN 1-56006-424-2 (alk. paper)
    1. Belleau Wood, Battle of, 1918—Juvenile literature.
    [1. Belleau Wood, Battle of, 1918. 2. World War, 1914–1918—Campaigns.]
    I. Title. II. Series.
D545.B4R53 1996
940.4'34—dc20
                95-31680
                CIP
                AC

Contents

Foreword   6

Chronology of Events   8

Introduction: America Enters the War   9

Chapter 1: Glory and Fortune   18

Chapter 2: "Retreat, Hell. We Just Got Here!"   32

Chapter 3: Facing Belleau Wood   40

Chapter 4: Hill 142   50

Chapter 5: Foothold in the Forest   59

Chapter 6: Devil Dogs   70

Chapter 7: Mustard Gas and Raw Guts   79

Chapter 8: "Belleau Woods Now U.S. Marine Corps Entirely"   89

Afterword: *Bois de la Brigade de Marine*   97

Glossary   103

For Further Reading   105

Works Consulted   106

Index   108

Picture Credits   111

About the Author   112

Foreword

Almost everyone would agree with William Tecumseh Sherman that war "is all hell." Yet the history of war, and battles in particular, is so fraught with the full spectrum of human emotion and action that it becomes a microcosm of the human experience. Soldiers' lives are condensed and crystallized in a single battle. As Francis Miller explains in his *Photographic History of the Civil War* when describing the war wounded, "It is sudden, the transition from marching bravely at morning on two sound legs, grasping your rifle in two sturdy arms, to lying at nightfall under a tree with a member forever gone."

Decisions made on the battlefield can mean the lives of thousands. A general's pique or indigestion can result in the difference between life and death. Some historians speculate, for example, that Napoleon's fateful defeat at Waterloo was due to the beginnings of stomach cancer. His stomach pain may have been the reason that the normally decisive general was sluggish and reluctant to move his troops. And what kept George McClellan from winning battles during the Civil War? Some scholars and contemporaries believe that it was simple cowardice and fear. Others argue that he felt a gut-wrenching unwillingness to engage in the war of attrition that was characteristic of that particular conflict.

Battle decisions can be magnificently brilliant and horribly costly. At the Battle of Thaspus in 47 B.C., for example, Julius Caesar, facing a numerically superior army, shrewdly ordered his troops onto a narrow strip of land bordering the sea. Just as he expected, his enemy thought he had accidentally trapped himself and divided their forces to surround his troops. By dividing their army, his enemy had given Caesar the strategic edge he needed to defeat them. Other battle orders result in disaster, as in the case of the Battle at Balaklava during the Crimean War in 1854. A British general gave the order to attack a force of withdrawing enemy Russians. But confusion in relaying the order resulted in the 670 men of the Light Brigade's charging in the wrong direction into certain death by heavy enemy cannon fire. Battles are the stuff of history on the grandest scale—their outcomes often determine whether nations are enslaved or liberated.

Moments in battles illustrate the best and worst of human character. In the feeling of terror and the us-versus-them attitude that accompanies war, the enemy can be dehumanized and treated with a contempt that is considered repellent in times of peace. At Wounded Knee, the distrust and anticipation of violence that grew between the Native Americans and American soldiers led to the senseless killing of ninety men, women, and children. And who can forget My Lai, where the deaths of old men, women, and children at the hands of American soldiers shocked an America already disillusioned with the Vietnam War. The murder of six million Jews will remain burned into the human conscience forever as the measure of man's inhumanity to man. These horrors cannot be forgotten. And yet, under the terrible conditions of battle, one can find acts of bravery, kindness, and altruism. During the Battle of Midway, the members of Torpedo Squadron 8, flying in hopelessly antiquated planes and without the benefit of air protection from fighters, tried bravely to fulfill their mission—to destroy the *Kido Butai,* the Japanese Carrier Striking Force. Without air support, the squadron was immediately set upon by Japanese fighters. Nevertheless, each bomber tried valiantly to hit his target. Each failed. Every man but one died in the effort. But by keeping the Japanese fighters busy, the squadron bought time and delayed further Japanese fighter attacks. In the aftermath of the Battle of Isandhlwana in South Africa in 1879, a force of thousands of Zulu warriors trapped a contingent of British troops in a small trading post. After repeated bloody attacks in which many died on both sides, the Zulus, their final victory certain, granted the remaining British their lives as a gesture of respect for their bravery. During World War I, American troops were so touched by the fate of French war orphans that they took up a collection to help them. During the Civil War, soldiers of the North and South would briefly forget that they were enemies and share smokes and coffee across battle lines during the endless nights. These acts seem all the more dramatic, more uplifting, because they indicate that people can continue to behave with humanity when faced with inhumanity.

Lucent Books' Battles Series highlights the vast range of the human character revealed in the ordeal of war. Dramatic narrative describes in exciting and accurate detail the commanders, soldiers, weapons, strategies, and maneuvers involved in each battle. Each volume includes a comprehensive historical context, explaining what brought the parties to war, the events leading to the battle, what factors made the battle important, and the effects it had on the larger war and later events.

The Battles Series also includes a chronology of important dates that gives students an overview, at a glance, of each battle. Sidebars create a broader context by adding enlightening details on leaders, institutions, customs, warships, weapons, and armor mentioned in the narration. Every volume contains numerous maps that allow readers to better visualize troop movements and strategies. In addition, numerous primary and secondary source quotations drawn from both past historical witnesses and modern historians are included. These quotations demonstrate to readers how and where historians derive information about past events. Finally, the volumes in the Battles Series provide a launching point for further reading and research. Each book contains a bibliography designed for student research, as well as a second bibliography that includes the works the author consulted while compiling the book.

Above all, the Battles Series helps illustrate the words of Herodotus, the fifth-century B.C. Greek historian now known as the "father of history." In the opening lines of his great chronicle of the Greek and Persian Wars, the world's first battle book, he set for himself this goal: "To preserve the memory of the past by putting on record the astonishing achievements both of our own and of other peoples; and more particularly, to show how they came into conflict."

Chronology of Events

1870–1871

Franco–Prussian War

1914

June 28   Austro-Hungarian archduke Francis Ferdinand and his wife, Sophie, assassinated by a Serbian terrorist.

August 3   Germany declares war on France.

August 4   England declares war on Germany; United States declares neutrality.

1915

May 7   German submarine sinks *Lusitania*.

1916

December 12   Germany announces willingness to enter peace negotiations with Allies.

1917

January 9   Kaiser Wilhelm II orders unrestricted submarine warfare.

January 19   German foreign minister Zimmerman sends telegram to German ambassador in Mexico proposing an anti-American alliance between Germany and Mexico.

February 3   German submarine sinks American cargo ship *Housatonic*.

March 16   German submarines torpedo American ships *City of Memphis* and *Illinois*.

April 2   President Woodrow Wilson asks U.S. Congress to declare war on Germany.

April 6   U.S. Congress declares war on Germany.

May 7   U.S. secretary of war Newton D. Baker names Major General John J. "Black Jack" Pershing to command American Expeditionary Force (AEF) in France.

June 14   American Expeditionary Force sails for France.

June 26   Advance guard of 5th Marines lands in France.

October 5   First elements of 6th Marines arrive in France.

October 23   5th and 6th Marine Regiments join to form 4th Marine Brigade, which then forms part of U.S. 2d Division.

November 8   Major General Omar Bundy arrives in France and assumes command of U.S. 2d Division.

1918

March 21   Major General Erich F. W. Ludendorff launches the Somme Offensive, first of several German offenses calculated to win the war for Germany.

April 9   Ludendorff launches Lys Offensive.

April 12   Germans lob gas shells on 6th Marines near Verdun.

May 27   Ludendorff mounts Aisne Offensive.

May 31   U.S. 3d Division holds Germans at Château-Thierry.

June 1   Château-Thierry falls to 231st German Infantry Division; U.S. 2d Division moves on line north of Le Thiolet.

June 2   Brigadier General James G. Harbord strengthens marine positions and orders marines to hold the line at all hazards.

June 3   Germans advance on Marigny and Lucy and occupy Belleau Wood.

June 3–4   German artillery blasts marines for two days.

June 4   Ludendorff calls off Aisne Offensive; General Bundy officially takes charge of American sector in vicinity of Belleau Wood.

June 5   German Corps Conta fails to advance on marine positions and is ordered to prepare defensive positions; General Bundy orders General Harbord's 4th Marine Brigade to counterattack along marine front; American-French artillery commence preparation fire.

June 6   Marines launch early morning attack on Hill 142 and late-afternoon assault on Belleau Wood.

June 7   Marines occupy Bouresches, Hill 142, and southern part of Belleau Wood.

June 8   Marines repulse German counterattack; Germans, in turn, repulse marine counterattack.

June 9   French and Americans bombard Belleau Wood with all-day artillery barrage.

June 10   Marines advance almost to center of Belleau Wood.

June 11   Marines penetrate German central defense line; Germans stop marines short of northern section of wood.

June 12   Germans halt marine advance with gas attack.

June 13   German counterattacks at Bouresches and in northern part of Belleau Wood fail.

June 13–15   Germans inflict heavy casualties on marines with high-explosive and mustard-gas shells.

June 15   4th Marine Brigade relieved by 7th Infantry Regiment of the U.S. 3d Division.

June 16–22   Germans hold U.S. 7th Infantry Regiment in place.

June 23   Part of the 4th Marine Brigade returns to Belleau Wood and resumes offensive.

June 24   Remainder of 4th Marine Brigade returns to front lines and drives Germans from northern part of wood; "Belleau Woods Now U.S. Marine Corps Entirely."

July 4   French honor Americans in Paris.

INTRODUCTION

America Enters the War

Europe started down the road to the Great War, as World War I was first called, during the last quarter of the nineteenth century. After defeating France in the Franco-Prussian War of 1870–1871, Germany, under Kaiser Wilhelm II, set out to establish itself as a world power. Germany's quest for power and influence challenged Great Britain's world supremacy and threatened France, which was still smarting from the loss of the Alsace-Lorraine region to the Germans in 1871. An atmosphere of competition and mounting tensions among nations pervaded Europe by the end of the century.

In the early 1900s, Austria began to fear Serbian expansion and the threat it posed to Austria's own Slavic lands. Then Russia grew alarmed over German and Austrian political and economic intentions toward the Balkans and Turkey. This string of conflicting national interests produced an accelerated arms race and induced nations to form alliances.

The Central Powers of Germany and Austria-Hungary (later joined by Turkey and Bulgaria) aligned themselves against the Allies of France, Russia, Serbia, Great Britain, and Belgium (which were later joined by Italy, Rumania, Portugal, Montenegro, Japan, Australia, the United States, and twenty other countries). Nations of each side sought through a position of unified strength to render war unacceptable to

Germany's victory over France in the Franco-Prussian War prefigured World War I by giving rise to Germany's quest for worldwide power.

The Franco-Prussian War

Rivalries, quarrels, skirmishes, and wars between and among nations have tormented Europe and its people throughout history. Resentments and hatreds fostered by centuries of contention among European nations contributed greatly to the causes of World War I. Most historians, however, select 1870 as a convenient and limiting starting point from which to analyze the origins of the Great War.

In mid-1870, the Prussians, under Chancellor Otto von Bismarck, tried to install a Hohenzollern (German dynastic family) noble on the Spanish throne. Emperor Napoleon III of France felt threatened by the possibility of a Prussian-Spanish two-front war against France. Assured by his military advisers that the French army was invincible, Napoleon initiated what he believed to be an inevitable war. France declared war on Prussia on July 15, 1870. Both countries mobilized rapidly. German mobilization (by the North German Confederation under Prussian leadership) and troop deployment followed a well-directed plan taking advantage of the railway network. French mobilization was disorderly and incomplete. The stronger, better-led German army humiliated the French army in less than ten months, taking Napoleon III prisoner and crushing France's Second Republic.

From September 1870 to January 1871, the Prussians laid siege to Paris, until the starvation-plagued French capital surrendered. The fighting continued in France's provinces until an armistice was declared and both sides signed the Treaty of Frankfurt on May 10, 1871.

Under terms of the treaty, the French agreed to pay a one-billion-dollar indemnity and remained occupied by the Germans until it was paid. Also, the Germans annexed the northern French provinces of Alsace and Lorraine, despite the objections of Bismarck. The German chancellor feared that the French would never forgive the loss of their land, but finally yielded to the uncompromising insistence of the German army.

Prophetically, Field Marshal Helmuth von Moltke, the great German strategist and commander of the army, said, "What our sword has won in half a year our sword must guard for half a century."

Moltke was almost right. Out of the blood and thunder of the Franco-Prussian War rose a German empire and the Third French Republic. Seven years shy of a half century, the two powers would clash again. And a world would join them in battle.

the other side. Rather than maintaining the status quo, or existing state of affairs, however, the alliances served only to heighten hostilities among the nations of Europe.

Germany increased the ranks of its standing army to more than two million men by 1914. France and Russia expanded their armies to more than a million each, while Austria and the British Empire assembled almost a million each. In total, nearly six million men stood at arms in the spring of 1914.

It then seemed inevitable that those arms would clash, as indicated by the American diplomat Colonel Edward M. House reporting from Germany: "Everybody's nerves are tense. It only requires a spark to set things off." That spark came on June 28, 1914, in Sarajevo, the capital of the Austrian province of Bosnia.

Archduke Francis Ferdinand, heir to the Austro-Hungarian throne, and his wife, Sophie, were gunned down in an open carriage by a Serbian assassin. Europe erupted in a war to end war.

On July 28, exactly one month after the murders in Sarajevo, Austria-Hungary declared war on Serbia. Russia started deploying troops along the German border. Germany responded by declaring war on Russia and its ally France. Britain entered the war when Germany invaded Belgium to outflank France. And so it went. Aligned nations acted and reacted to uphold the terms of alliances that had been set in place to preserve peace.

In London on August 3—the eve of Britain's entry into the war—British foreign secretary Sir Edward Grey watched from his window with a friend as the lights were being lit in the street below. "The lamps are going out all over Europe," he said. "We shall not see them lit again in our lifetime."

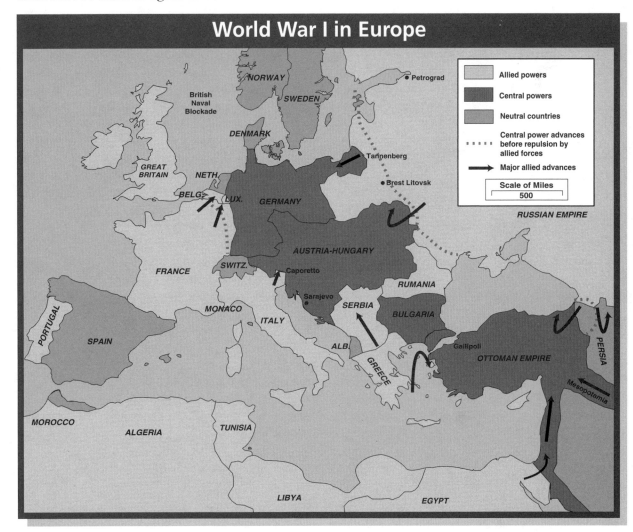

Slayings at Sarajevo

The archduke Ferdinand and his wife prepare to enter their car after leaving the Hotel de Ville in Sarajevo. This photo was taken minutes before Ferdinand's assassination.

The double assassination of Archduke Francis Ferdinand, heir to the Austro-Hungarian throne, and his wife, Sophie, provided the principal nations of Europe with an excuse for war. Although the origins and root causes of World War I went back several decades, the slayings at Sarajevo lit the fuse under a European powder keg of conflicting national aims and interests in 1914. As is often the case with monumental events in history, chance played a role.

On June 28, 1914, seven young Serbian nationalists arrived in Sarajevo, the capital of the Austrian province of Bosnia. A teacher, a printer, a carpenter, and four students, they came as self-proclaimed patriots in the company of horrid intent. With them, they carried Belgian pistols, crude hand bombs, and cyanide capsules—the last to take their own lives if necessary. The young Serbs had come to murder the archduke, whose policies they believed stood in the way of a greater Serbia.

A festive air prevailed in the city that morning. Sarajevo was celebrating the Feast of Saint Vitus, marking the rebirth of Serbia after its victory over the Turks in the sixteenth century. Crowds of noisy people lined streets bathed in bright sunlight and bedecked with colorful banners. Down one such street rode Archduke Ferdinand and Sophie in an open limousine. The seven Serbs blended into the crowd to take up prearranged stations and await their target. One of the would-be assassins threw his bomb at the royal pair but missed. Five of the other Serbs lost their nerve at the crucial moment. Pure chance then intervened to guide the fortunes of both royalty and rebel.

The driver of the Archduke's car made a wrong turn and drove the open limousine to within five feet of Gavrilo Princip, the seventh Serb conspirator. Princip, a frail youth afflicted with tuberculosis, did not fail his murderous task. His pistol snapped twice at point-blank range. One bullet struck archduke Ferdinand in the neck. The other lodged in Sophie's stomach. Blood spurted from the Archduke's mouth. "For heaven's sake, what's happened to you?" Sophie cried, then collapsed in a heap.

Her husband pleaded, "Sophie dear, Sophie dear, don't die! Stay alive for our children." But she was already dead. Archduke Ferdinand died a few minutes later. Their deaths triggered the start of a war that would claim ten million more lives over the next four years. Princip died in prison of tuberculosis in 1918.

Germans Sink the *Lusitania*

On August 4, 1914, across the broad Atlantic from Europe's strife, President Woodrow Wilson proclaimed American neutrality. He later told Americans: "We must be impartial in thought as well as in action, must put a curb on our sentiments." Before the war broke out in Europe, the United States had enjoyed friendly relations with countries on both sides of the conflict, so keeping a neutral status came easily to Americans at first.

As a neutral nation, the United States was prohibited from shipping war matériel to either side. But nothing in the rules of war prevented American manufacturers from *selling* to any nation with ships docking at American ports of call. Britain, with the largest navy in the world, benefited twice over by these limits: British freighters hauled tons of matériel out of American ports, while British warships turned away or sank most of the German ships heading for American destinations.

Britain next established a naval blockade against Germany and began stopping and seizing ships bound for German ports with contraband items. The British first defined contraband as war matériel—arms, ammunition, and the like. But when Germany responded with a blockade of its own against Britain, using submarines rather than surface ships, the British expanded their definition of contraband to include food supplies. Germany's Kaiser Wilhelm II then declared all goods moving toward Britain as contraband and designated British waters as a combat zone. He warned that enemy merchant ships found within the zone "would be destroyed without it always being possible to warn the crews and passengers." He failed to mention that his submarines might have a problem distinguishing between enemy and neutral merchant ships.

On May 7, 1915, a German submarine torpedoed the British liner *Lusitania*. The proud vessel sank within eighteen minutes, carrying 1,198 people to the bottom, including 128 American citizens. Americans were shocked and outraged by the sinking, even though the Germans had warned Americans not to book passage on the *Lusitania* and despite the fact that the liner had been carrying guns and munitions for the Allies. Until then, American public opinion had remained strictly

When the Germans torpedoed the Lusitania, *killing 128 Americans, U.S. public opinion toward the war shifted abruptly from neutral sentiments to firm, pro-British or anti-German feelings.*

neutral, favoring neither the British nor the Germans. American sentiments now shifted abruptly to firm pro-British or anti-German feelings, but not firm enough to make most Americans want to intervene in the war.

The Zimmermann Telegram

In that regard, President Wilson, a person dedicated to world peace, wanted desperately to keep the United States out of the war. He won reelection in 1916 with a campaign slogan of "He kept us out of war." After his reelection, Wilson tried hard to mediate a peace agreement in Europe. On December 12, 1916, Germany announced its willingness to negotiate with the Allies. Wilson's efforts appeared momentarily to be succeeding.

The Germans wanted to end the war quickly, while they still occupied (and could maintain claim to) Belgium and large parts of Italy, Russia, and France, and before Britain's blockade would force Germany's surrender. Recognizing Germany's motives in seeking a negotiated peace, the Allies refused to come quickly to the bargaining table and stated that Germany must first make full restitution and reparation. The Germans became evasive and the peace process stalled. Germany then resorted to its last hope for ending the war on its own terms.

On January 9, 1917, while German diplomats still talked of a peaceful settlement, the kaiser alerted his submarine fleet: "I order that unrestricted submarine warfare be launched with the greatest vigor on February 1."

In the U-boat, the Germans had a powerful tool to use against the superior British navy.

Over the Waves and Under the Sea

The British navy—the most powerful navy in the world in 1914—immediately established a naval blockade against Germany at the start of World War I. When a German offensive stalled at the Marne River in France in the first great battle of the war, the armies of both sides dug in and began a static war of attrition in the trenches. In a war where each side tries to wear down and outlast the other, breaking the British blockade became essential to Germany's survival.

Germany might have willingly challenged Britain's supremacy at sea had the German navy not been so woefully inadequate. The reality was that Germany stood no chance of matching the combined surface strength of the British and French navies. Incapable of challenging Britain on the ocean's surface, Germany resorted to unrestricted submarine warfare to establish a blockade of its own.

The German navy began the war with twenty-four submarines, or U-boats, as the Germans called them (short for *Unterseebooten*). By the end of 1915, nineteen U-boats had been sunk and fifty-four new ones added to Germany's undersea fleet.

Germany's U-boat commanders viewed their victims through a periscope and made little distinction between enemy and neutral shipping. Seldom would a commander risk surfacing in enemy seas. Thin-skinned, slow, and armed with only a small deck gun, the U-boat's vulnerability to Britain's more powerful surface ships dictated the submarine's serpentlike style of attack: sudden and unseen. Nor would the U-boats attempt to pick up enemy survivors, fearing to surface, as they did, and lacking space for additional passengers in their already cramped quarters. So, the U-boats ran silently and submerged, striking without warning or mercy.

When Britain complained that innocent women and children were being sent to the bottom with torpedoed ships, Germany shrugged and pointed to the women and children starved to death by the British blockade. By 1917, according to some claims, as many as 750,000 Germans died of starvation because of the blockade. But the world at large tended to ignore the internal sufferings of Germany caused by Britain's blockade. Rather, it was the unseen, unsuspected attacks of Germany's U-boats that shocked the world and outraged public opinion—especially in the United States, where strict neutrality gave way to pro-British sentiments.

The U-boats took a heavy toll. By April 1917, German submarines were destroying one of every four British ships at sea. Had British losses continued at that rate, Britain would have run out of ships by September of that year. Ultimately, however, the U-boat campaign failed when the United States entered the war. With America's help, Germany's undersea menace was neutralized and all but disappeared. Britannia ruled the waves once more.

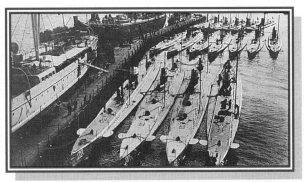

German U-boats lie in harbor during 1914.

Ten days later, the German foreign minister, Dr. Arthur Zimmermann, sent a coded telegram to the German ambassador in Mexico City. The message later became known as the infamous "Zimmermann telegram." It said:

> WE INTEND TO BEGIN UNRESTRICTED SUBMARINE WARFARE. WE SHALL ENDEAVOR TO KEEP THE UNITED STATES NEUTRAL. IN THE EVENT OF THIS NOT SUCCEEDING, WE MAKE MEXICO A PROPOSAL OF ALLIANCE ON THE FOLLOWING BASIS: MAKE WAR TOGETHER, MAKE PEACE TOGETHER, GENEROUS FINANCIAL SUPPORT, AND AN UNDERSTANDING ON OUR PART THAT MEXICO IS TO RECONQUER THE LOST TERRITORY IN TEXAS, NEW MEXICO, AND ARIZONA.

The British intercepted and decoded Zimmermann's message and informed President Wilson of its contents. Zimmermann's proposal was totally unrealistic. Mexico lacked any serious military capability and stood one step away from revolutionary upheaval. But the kaiser's acceleration of German submarine operations posed a genuine threat to both Allied and neutral ships at sea.

To Make the World Safe for Democracy

On February 3, the German submarine U-52 sank the American cargo ship *Housatonic* off the Scilly Islands, southwest of England. In Berlin, Foreign Minister Zimmermann conferred with the American ambassador and said, "Everything will be alright. America will do nothing, for President Wilson is for peace and nothing else. Everything will go on as before."

President Wilson gives voice to popular American sentiment when he asks Congress to declare war on Germany.

But it did not. Wilson informed Congress that same day that he was severing diplomatic relations with Germany. Two and a half years of wartime diplomacy ended. On March 16, German submarines torpedoed the American ships *City of Memphis* and *Illinois*. The last trace of American neutrality disappeared. President Wilson had tried to the limits of his power and ability to keep the United States out of the war, and he had failed.

A saddened Wilson, on April 2, 1917, went before Congress and asked for a declaration of war. "The world must be made safe for democracy," he told his emotion-charged audience, concluding:

It is a fearful thing to lead this great peaceful people into war, into the most terrible and disastrous of all wars, civilization itself seeming to be in the balance. But the right is more precious than peace. . . . The day has come when America is privileged to spend her blood and her might for the principles that gave her birth and happiness and the peace which she has treasured. God helping her, she can do no other.

On April 6, 1917, Congress declared war on Germany.

CHAPTER ONE

Glory and Fortune

Late in the afternoon of the sunny spring day of June 6, 1918, the marines of the 4th Marine Brigade gathered with bayonets fixed at the edge of a quarter-mile-long field of wheat. Beyond the field of lush green splashed with red poppies stood a tangle of forest, a half-mile wide and a little more than twice as long. An island of wood set in a sea of grassy meadowland, the forest was filled with rough underbrush, rocks and boulders, and dry ravines. Lengthening shadows within the wood now masked the eye's perception to the presence of thickly scattered nests of German machine guns and their lethal lanes of fire. Once a hunter's paradise, the French called this kidney-shaped, former game preserve Bois de Belleau. The marines would soon find cause to call it hell.

At 5 P.M. straight up, whistles shrieked all along the line of assembled marines. In unison, young platoon leaders stepped forward, pointed toward Belleau Wood, and shouted, "Follow me!" And elements of the 4th Marine Brigade stepped forth to honor their fighting tradition.

From a nearby rise, Colonel Albertus C. Catlin, commander of the 6th Marine Regiment, watched with pride. He would later write:

> It was one of the most beautiful sights I have ever witnessed. The battalion pivoted on its right, the left sweeping across the open ground in four waves, as steadily and correctly as though on parade. There were two companies of them, deployed in four skirmish lines, the men placed five yards apart and the waves 15–20 yards behind each other.

I say they went in as if on parade, and that is literally true. There was no yell or wild rush, but a deliberate forward march, with line at right dress. They walked at the regulation pace, because a man is of little use in a hand-to-hand bayonet struggle after a hundred yards dash. My hands were clenched and all my muscles taut as I watched that cool, intrepid, masterful defiance of the German spite. And still there was no sign of wavering or breaking.

Catlin watched his marines advance on Belleau Wood without regard to heavy fire around him. As his last elements reached the darkening fringes of the wood at 5:37 P.M., the colonel's luck ran out. A German bullet caught him in the chest, paralyzing his right side. Catlin survived an eight-hour ambulance ride to a Paris hospital and was subsequently sent home.

When the fighting on June 6 ended, casualty figures for the 4th Marine Brigade totaled 31 officers and 1,036 enlisted men. But the Marines had seized a foothold and were holding on in Belleau Wood.

Over There

On May 7, 1917, eleven months before the marines clashed with the Germans in Belleau Wood, Secretary of War Newton D. Baker called Major General John J. "Black Jack" Pershing to Washington. Pershing's diary entry for that day noted:

> Was informed by the Secretary of War that I was to command the American troops in France; and that I should prepare to leave for France as soon as possible.

Baker had selected the general, with the approval of President Woodrow Wilson, to command the American Expeditionary Force (AEF) abroad. General Pershing, a veteran of thirty-five years in the army and eleven years as a general officer, had become famous for leading an army expedition into Mexico in pursuit of the Mexican bandit Pancho Villa in 1916. Neither Baker nor Wilson had ever met the general. Newton's choice of Pershing, sight unseen, for this most important command was based on the general's outstanding service record and strength of character.

The American public enthusiastically approved Pershing's appointment to high command, as did then-Colonel James G. Harbord, Pershing's future chief of staff. Harbord later wrote that Pershing's background

Colonel Albertus C. Catlin (above), commander of the 6th Marine Regiment, was wounded in the Battle of Belleau Wood. Two key players in the U.S. war against the Germans are pictured below: General John J. Pershing commanded the American Expeditionary Force while Colonel James G. Harbord became Pershing's chief of staff.

epitomized the simple personal and professional record which was one factor in the selection of John J. Pershing to command the forces of the United States against the Central Powers. The other factor was his high character, reflected in a reputation for absolute integrity, strength, judgment, steadfastness, great discretion, and a loyalty beyond reproach.

After learning of his appointment, General Pershing met with U.S. Army chief of staff Major General Hugh Scott, who asked him to select units for a division to serve in France. Pershing selected the 16th, 18th, 26th, and the 28th Infantry Regiments, which together formed the 1st Division. The 1st Division, later nicknamed the Big Red One, became the advance guard of American forces in Europe.

When General Pershing received the orders establishing his authority, he found the fifth paragraph particularly noteworthy:

> You are directed to cooperate with the other countries . . . but in so doing the underlying idea must be kept in view that the forces of the United States are a separate and distinct component of the combined forces, the identity of which must be preserved.

Pershing would later receive much praise for not allowing American units to be merged with British or French units and placed under foreign command. In preserving the individuality of American fighting units, Pershing, in fact, was only following orders and the dictates of America's national and military heritage. But he attacked his task with the unswerving resolve of an English bulldog and the uncompromising zeal of a French rebel storming the Bastille. And for that, he deserves all credit.

The first elements of Black Jack Pershing's American Expeditionary Force—about fourteen thousand hastily assembled troops—sailed for France on June 14, 1917. Slightly more than two months after America's entry into the war, Americans were heading "Over There."

The 2d Division

Colonel Charles A. Doyen's 5th Marine Regiment, with 2,759 men, comprised one-fifth of the AEF that sailed for Europe on June 14. The 5th Marines also made up one-fifth of the entire U.S. Marine Corps, which started the war with 514 officers and 13,214 enlisted men. In the next seventeen months, the ranks of the corps would swell to 2,462 officers and 72,639 enlisted men.

Historians have often noted that rarely, if ever, has a nation been so totally unprepared for war as was the United States in 1917. Oddly, even though the army itself began the war with less than 135,000 men, initial War Department planning did not include using marines in land action against the enemy. But Major General George Barnett, the commandant of the Marine Corps,

was not one to sit idly by and watch the fighting from the sidelines. "I do not want the Marine Corps to be considered a police force," Barnett declared, insisting that his marines stood ready to fight alongside soldiers on the Western Front. The 5th Marines landed at Saint-Nazaire with the advance guard of the AEF on June 26.

Meanwhile, elements of Colonel Albertus C. Catlin's 6th Marines were forming at Quantico, Virginia, and Parris Island, South Carolina. Most of Catlin's marines were new men, many of whom had responded to Commandant Barnett's recruiting posters challenging America's youth to become "First to Fight." Of the 6th Marine Regiment, Catlin later wrote:

> The officers, from captain up, and 50 or so of the non-commissioned officers were old-time Marines, but the junior officers and all of the privates were new men. . . . 60 percent of the entire regiment—mark this—60 percent of them were college men. Two-thirds of one entire company came straight from the University of Minnesota. . . .

> Of our young lieutenants a large number were college athletes.

American soldiers enthusiastically embark for France. Unlike their Allied comrades, these Americans had not yet been tested by the brutal killing fields of Europe.

American soldiers perform maneuvers in preparation to fight in Europe.

Most of the marines of that day underwent training at Parris Island—a kind of hell on earth just off the South Carolina coast from Port Royal. A land populated mostly by shaved heads and sand fleas, Parris Island is a school for modern centurions, dedicated to turning boys into men and men into marines. In a letter home, one recruit, in bare-boned prose, deftly sketched the purpose and experience of a Parris Island education:

> The first day I was at camp I was afraid that I was going to die. The next two weeks my sole fear was that I wasn't going to die. And after that I knew I'd never die because I'd become so hard that nothing could kill me.

After completing a rigorous curriculum of physical conditioning, hand-to-hand combat, bayonet fighting, weapons training, classroom instruction on military subjects, close-order drill, and—most important—marksmanship, the toughened and disciplined graduates of Quantico and Parris Island boarded ship in Philadelphia and shipped out for France. The first elements of the 6th Marine Regiment began arriving in France on October 5, 1917.

Initially, neither the War Department nor General Pershing had asked for or wanted front-line assistance from the Marine Corps. Pershing, a dedicated army officer, placed little trust in the ability of marine "soldiers of the sea" to get the job done in the muck and mire of European land operations. At first, the AEF commander did his best to ignore the marines by assigning most of them to stevedore and routine guard duties upon their arrival in France. The marines had to fight for the chance to fight.

With the acute shortage of American combat units in France, coupled with increasing pressures from Congress and the president to use marines in combat roles, neither Pershing's headquarters nor the War Department could ignore the presence of nearly two marine regiments. On September 20, two weeks before the 6th Marines began arriving in France, the War Department authorized a marine brigade to replace the army brigade originally planned to form part of the U.S. 2d Division.

On October 23, the 5th and 6th Marine Regiments combined to form the 4th Marine Brigade and were soon strengthened by the addition of the 6th Marine Machine Gun Battalion. The 4th Marine Brigade then joined with the army's 3d Infantry Brigade and 2d Field Artillery Brigade to form the U.S. 2d Division, under the command of the newly promoted Brigadier General Charles A. Doyen, the senior marine in France. General Doyen, who had previously commanded the 5th Marines and then the 4th Marine Brigade, opened division headquarters in Bourmont, a village about 150 miles southeast of Paris. His new command was short-lived.

On November 8, 1917, Major General Omar Bundy, U.S. Army, arrived from the United States and replaced Doyen as commander of the 2d Division. Doyen resumed command of the 4th Marine Brigade.

Up Front at Last

Although the U.S. 1st Division was committed to battle on October 23, 1917, the 2d Division, with its marines, saw no action until the following March. In the interim, the marines underwent tough training in the various killing arts.

Commander of the 4th Marine Brigade, Charles A. Doyen. (Bottom, left) American soldiers head off to France after their arrival in Britain.

Combat training for marines commenced shortly after the arrival of their first contingents in September. Most marine units were attached temporarily to British or French units for instruction. Much of their training focused on trench warfare, recalled Lieutenant Colonel Frederic M. "Fritz" Wise, whose 2d Battalion, 5th Marines, trained with the crack 115th French Chasseurs Alpins—the famous Blue Devils. Wise later wrote:

> We dug a series of trenches. We took up the new method of bayonet fighting. Long lines of straw-stuffed figures hanging from a crossbeam between two upright posts were set up. The men fixed bayonets and charged them. British instructors, who had arrived shortly after us, stood over them and urged them on. . . . The British at that time were crazy about the bayonet. They knew it was going to win the war. The French were equally obsessed with the grenade. They knew *it* was going to win the war. So we also got a full dose of training in hand grenade throwing.

Following some interesting experiences learning how to fire the rifle grenade and the one-pounder, or 37mm gun, Wise related:

The infamous trenches of the Western Front, where most of World War I would be fought. The trenches made life hell for Germans and Allied soldiers alike.

The Way He Was

The Marine Corps has consistently instilled in its members a spirit, discipline, and professionalism that has enabled them to face the toughest challenges and prevail. A marine's training begins the moment he or she says "I do" to the oath of allegiance. It never ceases. Lieutenant Lemuel C. Shepherd, a future marine commandant, never forgot the training he received under his battalion commander, Lieutenant Colonel Frederic M. "Fritz" Wise, in the winter of 1917–1918. Shepherd later wrote:

> Colonel Wise really put it to us that winter. We were constantly on the alert. Sometimes at night we were called out without warning to make a hike in sub-zero weather. Around Christmas we marched to mock trenches where we spent three days in assimilated trench warfare. It was rugged duty but we learned a great deal and we became tough as nails. I personally learned something about Colonel Wise, whom we all regarded as something of an ogre.

Colonel Wise, who demanded strict obedience in his battalion, later confided his reasons to Shepherd during a private talk:

> Shepherd, you've been with me some time now and you know I'm considered a martinet [one who demands strict discipline]. I know that you youngsters fuss because I insist on meticulous obedience of my orders. Some of them seem petty to you—the making up of bunks to regulation, the correct uniform, my inspecting every rifle in the battalion. I insist on these little things because they make the big things. One of these days we'll be in combat and the only way we can win is by strict and unqualified obedience of orders. In combat you won't have time to think and deliberate over an order. You will have to execute it immediately without questioning your superior. When we go into battle this battalion will be so trained that there will never be any question about our disobeying an order or not carrying it out to the best of our ability.

Shepherd concluded:

> It was a talk I remembered all my life. It was the only time he ever showed another side to me, the only time he explained that he had a purpose for being the way he was.

We were put through a series of shows to teach us how trench raids were conducted and repelled. We had a gas mask drill and were put through a gas chamber. We were given a workout with those damnable French Chauchat automatic rifles. . . . The men worked their heads off at all this new stuff. They assembled and dismounted machine guns, learned the names of the parts and how to repair them. They made wire entanglements and dugouts. They looked upon the French instructors as gods, for they knew they were being trained by veteran troops.

After nearly a year at war, the United States still had only six divisions and fewer than three hundred thousand troops in

France, but fifty thousand more were now arriving every month. The marines finally went on-line for the first time in mid-March in a so-called quiet sector near Verdun. No one told the Germans to keep the peace, however, as the marines would soon discover. That was all right with the marines, who, by then, were sick of training and ready for action. They were delighted to be up front at last.

Rites of Passage

On March 21, Major General Erich F. W. Ludendorff, the deputy chief of the German General Staff, launched the first of several offensives calculated to win the war for Germany before the United States could tip the balance of power in Europe. The Germans struck the British at Amiens in the Somme Offensive. On April 9, Ludendorff initiated the Lys Offensive, again hitting the British, this time on a narrower front in Flanders.

Three days later, the Germans lobbed deadly gas shells on 74th Company, 6th Marines, near Verdun, forcing evacuation of the entire company because of faulty or misplaced gas masks.

Three key German officials confer over battle plans. At left is General von Hindenburg, in the middle, Kaiser Wilhelm, and at right is Major General Erich F.W. Ludendorff, the deputy chief of the German General Staff.

During and after the evacuation, a total of forty marines succumbed to the slow, lingering, excruciatingly painful effects of the gas.

Of the nearly fifty-eight thousand American gas casualties in World War I, 26,828 came from mustard gas. The death of its victims sometimes took as long as four or five weeks. One nurse wrote:

> I wish those people who write so glibly about this being a holy war and the orators who talk so much about going on no matter how long the war lasts, and what it may mean, could see a case—to say nothing of ten cases—of mustard gas in its early stages—could see the poor things burnt and blistered all over with great mustard-coloured suppurating blisters [blisters forming or discharging pus], with blind eyes . . . all sticky and stuck together, and always fighting for breath, with voices a mere whisper, saying that their throats are closing and they know they will choke.

During their brief stint on-line, 45th Company, 5th Marines, and 74th and 84th Companies, 6th Marines, all successfully repelled German raids on their positions. For most of the marines, it was their first experience in harm's way. They were shelled, gassed, attacked, killed, wounded, and some were taken prisoner. They met the *Boche*—the French slang term for German soldiers—and stood firm, returning German aggressions in full measure. By the time they were suddenly withdrawn from the Verdun vicinity in May, the marines had completed their rites of passage in the trenches and shown their willingness to fight. In so doing, they had won the esteem of Black Jack Pershing. They could now take their place among front-line veterans.

In a training exercise (above), U.S. soldiers demonstrate the effects of gas shells, which blistered the lungs and air passages, causing a slow and agonizing death. (Below) German infantry attack Allied lines in the spring of 1918 before the American counterattack that followed the Château-Thierry battle.

A Quick and Fateful Decision

Ludendorff mounted his third offensive of the spring at the Aisne River, attacking General Denis A. Duchêne's French 6th Army at Chemin des Dames on May 27. The U.S. 3d Division held the Germans at Château-Thierry on May 31. Meanwhile, the U.S. 2d Division moved up along the Paris-Metz road, through long lines of French 6th Army troops and civilians fleeing from the front.

A Bitter Truth

The men of the 4th Marine Brigade might have felt less eager to join the fighting on the Western Front had they known more of the horror and desolation to be found there. Paul Nash, a British war artist whose job it was to capture the war on canvas, wrote word pictures of the war's setting as vivid and evocative as any of his paintings. In his deeply felt desire to convey the truth of the war to others, Nash wrote:

> It is unspeakable, godless, hopeless. I am no longer an artist interested and curious, I am a messenger who will bring back word from the men who are fighting to those who want the war to go on for ever. Feeble, inarticulate, will be my message, but it will have a bitter truth, and it may burn their lousy souls.

With rare eloquence and deft strokes, using words in lieu of oils or watercolors, Nash painted the truth of the Western Front:

> No pen or drawing can convey this country—the normal setting of the battles taking place day and night, month after month. Evil and the incarnate fiend alone can be master of this war, and no glimmer of God's hand is seen anywhere. Sunset and sunrise are blasphemous, they are mockeries to man, only the black rain out of the bruised and swollen clouds all through the bitter black of night is fit atmosphere in such a land. The rain drives on, the stinking mud becomes evilly yellow, the shellholes fill up with green-white water, the roads and tracks are covered in inches of slime, the black dying trees ooze and sweat and shells never cease. They alone plunge overhead, tearing away the rotting tree stumps . . . annihilating, maiming, maddening, they plunge into the grave which is this land; one huge grave, and cast upon it the poor dead. It is unspeakable, godless, hopeless.

Paul Nash survived World War I and lived to convey the truth of another war twenty years later.

Again and again, weary French soldiers passing through the fresh American troops said, *"La guerre est finie"* ("The war is ended"). And over and over marines replied, *"Pas fini"* ("It is not ended"). The sector soon became known as the Pas Fini sector.

Château-Thierry fell to the 231st German Infantry Division on June 1. But when confronted by American machine-gun fire, the still-advancing Germans swerved to their right, capturing the village of Vaux and occupying Belleau Wood. Major General Jean M. J. Degoutte, commander of the French XXI Corps and Allied operations in that sector, called for American help. The 9th Infantry Regiment, of the U.S. 3d Brigade, answered his call. Degoutte positioned the regiment between the Paris-Metz highway and the Marne River facing Vaux, then called urgently for a second American regiment.

General Bundy, U.S. 2d Division commander, ordered recently promoted Brigadier General James G. Harbord, U.S. Army, now commander of the 4th Marine Brigade, to send in a regiment at Belleau Wood. General Doyen, the brigade's original commander, had fallen terminally ill and had been sent home. Lacking a marine general to succeed Doyen, General Pershing had assigned command of the 4th Marine Brigade to Harbord, his former chief of staff.

Pershing warned the marines' new commander, "You are to have charge of the finest body of troops in France, and if they fail to live up to that reputation, I shall know whom to blame."

On June 1, Harbord moved the 6th Marine Regiment up to the left of the 9th Infantry and deployed the marines to the north from Le Thiolet on the Paris-Metz road. The marines positioned themselves with Major Thomas Holcomb's 2d Battalion on the right, Major Maurice Shearer's 1st Battalion on the left to the north, and Major Berton W. Sibley's 3d Battalion in reserve. The 5th Marine and U.S. 23d Infantry Regiments took up support positions.

Earlier, when General Bundy had ordered General Harbord to commit a regiment of marines to the action, Harbord had replied, "I'd be glad to, General. But I hope you won't split my brigade in its first action. Can't you let the Paris-Metz road be the

German Offensives, 1918

NETH.

Dunkirk
Calais
Flanders

BELGIUM

Boulogne

GERMANY

Lys R.

②

Somme R.

Amiens

Centigny

Montdidier

① Somme Offensive, March 21

② Lys Offensive, April 9

③ Aisne Offensive, May 27

Scale of Miles
50

LUX.

③

Aisne R.

Oise R.

Soissons

Seine R.
Paris

Château-Thierry

Life in the Trenches

Except for the first and last months of World War I, the fighting was confined almost exclusively to the trenches, where the men of the infantry, in a constant struggle for survival, fought the elements, fatigue, hunger, fear, boredom, rats, lice, and an unrelenting enemy. The infantry made up one-half of the armies on both sides and incurred 80 percent of the war's casualties. War in the trenches took a staggering toll of human lives. In the First Battle of the Somme (June–November 1916) alone, in grim testament to the machine gun's rule, British losses totaled 420,000; French, 195,000. German losses, at 650,000, exceeded the combined total of British and French losses.

Intricate trench systems of opposing sides defined the Western Front that stretched from southern Belgium to Switzerland. Similar but less sophisticated trench systems scribed the Italian, Balkan, and eastern fronts. As a rule, battalion-size units of some one thousand men (in theory) would occupy a section of trench line and remain at the front for about five days, with each day divided into six four-hour periods. While in the trenches, a soldier could expect to sleep about four hours a day, unless interrupted by an emergency "stand to," or some other unpleasant urgency.

Each soldier "stood to" for two nonconsecutive periods every day, standing watch on the firing step of the trench in full battle dress—webbing equipment (canvas cartridge belts, packs, etc.), bayonet and scabbard, entrenching tool (shovel), gas mask, steel helmet, and canteen. Two additional nonconsecutive periods were designated as working periods, for digging and repairing trenches, duck boards (slatted flooring laid on wet, muddy, or cold trench bottoms), dugouts (quarters dug in the side of a trench), and filling and laying sandbags. Although there was often little to be done during these stand-to and working periods, no sleeping was permitted.

Nor was sleeping allowed during group (usually platoon) rest periods, when the soldiers sat in dugouts with their backs against the wall—again in battle dress, except for their packs, which they were allowed to remove. A form of organized dozing frequently occurred, however, with one man designated as sentry to warn the others of any approaching officers.

Some of the more challenging front-line tasks—repairing barbed-wire entanglements, patrolling, and attempting to capture prisoners in no-man's-land (the land between opposing trench lines)—were conducted at night. Continual star-shell bursts lit up the front at night, illuminating the work and exposing the worker, with a stark intensity that turned mud to silver and shell holes into earthbound craters of the moon.

Once relieved, front-line battalions would spend one to two weeks in reserve trenches or camps and then repeat the cycle.

A marine receives first aid where he has fallen in the trenches on March 22, 1918. He will be evacuated to a hospital in the rear of the trenches.

dividing line between the brigades, so that I may place my regiments now north of the road?"

The generals had then agreed that the marine brigade would fight as a unit north of the highway; the 3d Infantry Brigade would do likewise south of the road. From their "spur of the moment decision came the alignment and the tremendous consequence," army historian S. L. A. Marshall wrote later, "to the glory of the United States Marines, to the fortunes of the two brigades, and to the future of the world."

The town of Château-Thierry lies in ruins after the German retreat on July 27, 1918. Marine machine-gun fire caused the Germans to abandon the town and move to occupy Belleau Wood.

CHAPTER TWO

"Retreat, Hell. We Just Got Here!"

On the evening of June 1, the Germans opened a hole in the French line to the left front of the marines. General Bundy sent Colonel Paul Malone's 23d Infantry Regiment, Major Julius S. Turrill's 1st Battalion, 5th Marines, part of the 5th Machine Gun Battalion, and a company of engineers to plug the gap in the French defenses, slightly more than six miles away.

General Harbord strengthened his marine positions on the morning of June 2, inserting Lieutenant Colonel Frederic M. Wise's 2d Battalion, 5th Marines, between Major Turrill's 1st Battalion, 5th Marines, on the left, and Major Shearer's 1st Battalion, 6th Marines, to the right. Major Benjamin S. Berry's 3d Battalion, 5th Marines, remained in reserve behind Turrill and Wise.

Marines Dig In

Colonel Wendell C. Neville, regimental commander of the 5th Marines, arrived at the front shortly before noon and directed Wise to establish a defensive line between Veuilly Wood and Les Mares Farm. "The French are holding from the railroad on your front," Neville told Wise, a chunky, bulldoglike Virginian, "but we don't expect them to stick. If you don't hurry, the Germans will get there before you do. And when you get there, you stick! Never mind how many French come through you."

Before one o'clock that afternoon, Wise's battalion found itself thinly stretched over a two-mile front. German light artillery—77mm "whiz-bangs" and 88mm "quick-Dicks"—began pounding them at once. Lieutenant E. D. Cooke, an army officer assigned to Wise's battalion, would later write:

Shells stuck in the treetops and fragments glittered in the air, like a shoal of small silver fish. The blow was quick, sudden, destructive, and eleven of our men went down. One or two cried out in surprised pain, but four lay inert and silent. Faces turned white and the company showed a tendency to huddle and mill about.

"Get going!" Captain Wass [company commander of 18th Company] sprang at them, a regular terrier for action. "What do you think this is, a kid's game. Move out!"

We scuttled through the woods, ducked and dodged as more shells pounded a shallow trench to our right, and then threw ourselves face down in the north edge of the Bois de Veuilly. To our front was a wheat field falling away gently into a narrow little valley and rising again to a forward slope some eight hundred yards ahead.

The exposed marines hastened to dig in. Since engineers had yet to arrive with entrenching tools, the marines dug with bayonets, mess kits, spoons, and anything else that would make a hole.

Lem Shepherd, second in command of Captain John Blanchfield's 55th Company, 5th Marines, described their individual foxholes, dug in on a line fronting Les Mares Farm, as "little scooped-up hollows similar to a grave but about a foot deep, with earth piled up in front for a parapet."

As the marines settled into their holes to await whatever was to come next, their thoughts turned to their empty stomachs.

German machine gunners line up on their target beneath a roadside tree. Machine-gun fire raked the American troops at Belleau Wood whenever they attempted to move from their positions.

Food now presented a problem to the hungry troops. Field rations had been eaten by then, and the mobile kitchens were still lagging far behind. Although some French rations were available, it took a strong stomach to tolerate the all-but-inedible fare. The main item on the French menu was canned, boiled, Argentine corned beef, called "monkey meat" by the marines. The meat had spoiled before being canned. To discerning marine noses the beef smelled like "a combination of coal oil and putrid mule." Most of the men could not gag it down and settled for rolling and smoking a succession of Bull Durham cigarettes to stave off hunger pangs.

Marines Ordered to Hold

During that afternoon, a captured German soldier disclosed that a fresh German division was preparing to attack the American right flank. Two regiments were to strike the Americans north of the Paris-Metz highway and one to the south. General Degoutte, the French corps commander who was still in overall command of the sector, ordered Major Benjamin S. Berry's 3d Battalion, 5th Marines, to move into a support position behind the junction of the 3d and 4th Brigades. General Bundy then withdrew Turrill's 1st Battalion, 5th Marines, to replace Berry's 3d Battalion, 5th Marines, behind Wise's 2d Battalion, 5th Marines.

The Americans now occupied a twelve-mile section of the front, extending from the 9th Infantry south of the highway, across the marine positions, and through to the 23d Infantry in the north. The thin marine line looked out upon rippling fields of grain, broken here and there by small clumps of trees. Incoming German artillery continued to pummel the marines, thinning their ranks further yet. Short of ammunition, hot food, and water, and aware that the worst was still to come, the marines could only sit and wait.

While the marines and soldiers of Bundy's 2d Division were establishing their positions to the north and south of the Paris-Metz highway, respectively, the Germans had been advancing toward them. In a move to extend the right flank of Corps Conta (named for its commander, General Richard von Conta) of General Max von Boehn's German 7th Army, General von Diepenbroick-Grüter's 10th Division attacked southwesterly toward Vaux and Bouresches. Attacking in the same general direction along the line of the Clignon Brook, General von Jacobi's 237th Division advanced between Bouresches and Torcy, and General von Wilhelmi's 197th Division moved forward between Torcy and Gandelu. By evening, the German 7th Army held a line from Vaux to Bouresches to Belleau and occupied Belleau Wood. The marines now faced the Germans across rolling fields in an irregular line from Hill 142 to Lucy-le-Bocage to Triangle Farm.

General Duchêne, still commanding the French 6th Army and retaining overall responsibility for the marine sector, dispatched a message to General Harbord: "Your men must hold the line at all hazards." A second message followed: "Have your men prepare entrenchments some hundreds of yards to rearward in case of need."

General Harbord would have none of it. Harbord passed Duchêne's two contradictory messages to his troops with his own curt rejection: "We will dig no trenches to fall back to. The Marines will hold where they stand."

"They Didn't Stand a Chance"

The next afternoon, June 3, the Germans advanced on Marigny and Lucy and moved on through Belleau Wood. Farther to the south, additional German divisions crossed the Marne. The French 43d Division counterattacked south of the Gandelu-Bussiares-Torcy sector to the left of the marine front. The French attack, weak and disorganized, bogged down quickly. But the revitalized French troops gave German front-line commanders reason to pause and become wary, which temporarily drained them of fresh momentum.

In the previous forty-eight hours, the Corps Conta had suffered more than two thousand casualties. The German offensive could not stand much more of the same and maintain its momentum. Although slowed by the renewed French resistance, the German 197th and 237th Divisions continued to advance, pushing south from Bussiares and Torcy, but now moving more cautiously.

Late that afternoon, extended lines of German soldiers with fixed bayonets crossed the open wheat fields to the marine front.

In true marine fashion, General Harbord refused to have his troops pull back from the position they had tried so hard to earn in Belleau Wood.

A German soldier lies dead in Belleau Wood, a silent testament to the gritty side of war.

Suddenly, German artillery opened up with a thunderous barrage of greater sound and force than any yet experienced by the marines. The marines huddled in their holes and waited in silence.

Several hundred yards in front of the marine lines, Lieutenant Lem Shepherd watched the advancing Germans from a hill with a commanding view and an excellent field of fire. "Shells were exploding all over the place," he wrote later. "One fell six feet to our front, a dud." Shepherd continued:

> The barrage was now passing to the rear. Behind it the Germans were beginning to appear. We watched them come. . . . Just over the crest of our hill there was a lone tree. I stood just in front of the tree where I could see and not be seen. About dusk the enemy began working around our hill. I gave the order to fire.

> We opened up with what we had. They countered with a machine gun. A bullet from the first blast caught me in the neck. I spun around and dropped to the ground. My first reaction was to see if I could spit. I wanted to know if the bullet had punctured my throat. I figured that if I could spit I was all right. I could spit. I crawled up beside my men. Several of them [fourteen total] had been hit but the rest kept firing. They fired until dark. Just after dark we fell back to our main line, bringing our wounded with us.

German infantry load a trench mortar in Belleau Wood. Such German ordnance rained mercilessly down upon the marines during the Battle of Belleau Wood.

Box Seats

On June 3, 1918, Colonel Albertus C. Catlin, commander of the 6th Marines, and his adjutant, Major Frank Evans, both viewed the front-line action from their newly established regimental post of command, a house in the little village of La Voie du Châtel. Evans later wrote that, from the second story of the farmhouse,

The house in the village of La Voie du Châtel that served as the marine headquarters.

> we had observation of the north, and when the Germans attacked at 5 P.M. we had a box seat. They were driving at Hill 165 from the north and northeast, and they came out, on a wonderfully clear day, in two columns across a wheat-field. From our distance it looked flat and green as a baseball field, set between a row of woods on the farther side, and woods and a ravine on the near side. We could see two thin brown columns advancing in perfect order until two thirds of the columns, we judged, were in view. . . .

> The rifle and machine gun fire were incessant and overhead the shrapnel was bursting. Then the shrapnel came on the target at each shot. It broke just over and just ahead of those columns and then the next bursts sprayed over the very green in which we could see the columns moving. It seemed for all the world that the green field had burst out in patches of white daisies where those columns were doggedly moving. And it did it again and again. . . .

> You couldn't begrudge a tribute to their pluck at that! Then, under that deadly fire and the barrage of rifle and machine gun fire, the Boches stopped. It was too much for any men. They burrowed in or broke to the cover of the woods. . . . The French, who were in support of the 5th [Marines], could not, and cannot today, grasp the rifle fire of the men. That men should fire deliberately and use their sights, and adjust their range, was beyond their experience. The rifle fire certainly figured heavily in the toll we took.

Colonel Catlin also recorded his impressions of the fighting that day:

> If the [perfect order of the] German advance had looked beautiful to me, that metal curtain that our Marines rang down on the scene was even more so. The German lines did not break; they were broken. . . . Three times they tried to re-form and break through that barrage, but they had to stop at last. The United States Marines had stopped them. Thus repulsed with heavy losses, they retired, but our fire was relentless; it followed them to their death.

Captain Lloyd Williams, company commander of 51st Company during the Battle of Belleau Wood. When asked to retreat, Williams uttered the now famous, "Retreat, hell. We just got here!"

To Shepherd's right, Captain Lloyd Williams, company commander of 51st Company, 2d Battalion, 5th Marines, watched the oncoming Germans draw as close to Paris as they had come since 1914. "We watched them come on," Williams said later. "A thousand yards, seven hundred, five hundred. I held our fire. Our sights were set for three hundred yards." His marines crouched low in their foxholes, their Springfield .03 and French Chauchat rifles loaded and locked, and waited. Four hundred and fifty, four hundred. . . .

And to the right of 51st Company, an unnamed machine gunner of Colonel Catlin's 6th Marines also held his fire and waited for the barrage to lift:

It lasted just an even hour and then Fritz [slang for German] came at us with blood in his eye. I estimated them at about 500 and they were in fairly compact masses. We waited until they got close, oh, very close. In fact, we let them think they were going to have a leadpipe cinch.

Oh, it was too easy; just like a bunch of cattle coming to slaughter.

I always thought it was rather a fearful thing to take a human life, but I felt a savage thrill of joy and I could hardly wait for the Germans to get close enough. And they came arrogant, confident in their power, to within 300 yards.

On orders, the young machine gunner opened fire:

Rat-tat-tat-tat full into them, and low down, oh! But it was good to jam down on the trigger, to feel her kick, to look out ahead, hand on the controlling wheel, and see the Heinies [slang for Germans] fall like wheat under the mower. They were brave enough, but they didn't stand a chance.

"A Miracle in the War"

A gap existed on both sides of Wise's thinly spread 2d Battalion, 5th Marines, when the German attack commenced. Because the marines had moved into position so hurriedly, communications problems plagued marine commanders from the start. Most of their posts of command (PCs) lacked telephones, which had not arrived from the rear. Communications were limited at first to runners. In the resulting confusion, Wise had failed to establish contact with either Malone's 23d Infantry to his left, or Shearer's 1st Battalion, 6th Marines, on his right.

Fortunately for Wise's battalion—and the Allied cause—the Germans attacked the center of Wise's strength and not his easily penetrable flanks. Wise described the action later:

Some of the key commanders of the Battle of Belleau Wood, including Frederic Wise (right) and General Doyen (left of Wise).

If ever there was a miracle in the war, that was it. With a wide front, much of it open, to pick and choose, the German attack had smashed squarely into the center of those lone two and a half miles we held. Had the same force hit either of our flanks, they could have crumpled us and cleaned us up.

I was in no position to exploit our success. The only thing in the world we could do was stick in our foxholes and hold that line. Out in front of us were Germans in unknown force. Both of our flanks remained unprotected. God alone knew how far back of us any support might be. But the Germans never attacked us again.

An Issue in Doubt

All that night, battle-weary, all-but-defeated French troops passed through marine positions. When a French major ordered Captain Lloyd Williams—company commander of Wise's 51st Company on the marine right—to withdraw, Williams replied, "Retreat, hell. We just got here!" Williams intended to stay for a while.

But the Germans were massing five divisions in front of the marines. The marines *had* stopped the German advance within forty miles of Paris. For *how long* remained an issue in doubt.

☆ ☆ ☆ ☆ ☆ ☆ ☆ ☆ ☆ ☆ ☆ ☆ ☆

CHAPTER THREE

Facing Belleau Wood

Scattered firefights and sniper fire continued during the early evening hours of June 3, while stretcher bearers from both sides crept and crawled about the woods and grassy fields collecting the dead and wounded. As the night wore on, small-arms fire gave way to the big guns. Exhausted poilus [slang term for French soldiers] from the French 43d Division filtered through the marine lines and completed their withdrawal under cover of darkness. At the same time, the French 167th Division moved up to replace their weary comrades.

The Corps Conta had failed to reach its assigned objectives, falling substantially short on its right flank. Worse, from von Conta's perspective, the day's fighting had cost him more than eight hundred casualties, and his corps had fallen back in disarray. At midnight on June 3, he ordered his division commanders to "fight for a position that is especially suited for defense." His order went on to state:

> The offensive spirit must be maintained, even though a temporary lull in the attack seems to exist. In the general picture of the operations, no halt or lull exists. We are the victors and will remain on the offensive. The enemy is defeated and the High Command will utilize this great success to the fullest extent.

As optimistic as von Conta's order sounded, the German commander still felt compelled to commit the 5th Guards, a reserve division, to his right flank. He further indicated:

The time for the attack will be ordered later. The attack will not occur before June 7. Reconnaissance and preparations will be started at once.

By "reconnaissance" von Conta meant continuing isolated attacks along his front. "Preparations" included rushing heavy artillery forward to supplement the shriek of 77s and 88s with the thunder of 150s and the giant 210mm *minenwerfers* (trench mortars). The German bombardment persisted throughout June 3 and 4, inflicting some two hundred casualties on the marines. General von Conta concluded his order by emphasizing:

> The main task of the commanders for the present is to reorganize their units and commanders to regain strict control of their troops again, and replace the shortage of officers, men and equipment. The temporary halt is further to be utilized to reorganize the service of supply and rearrange the rearward communications.

Sheltered in the rubble of a building, German soldiers are poised to fire deadly bursts of machine-gun rounds at the advancing enemy.

General von Conta's order clearly showed that he had come to realize that achieving his objectives might prove to be more difficult than he had anticipated at first. The Americans were tough.

General Erich Ludendorff called off the Lys Offensive on June 4. The Germans dug in along a line starting at Torcy and running roughly to Belleau Wood, to Le Thiolet, and ending at Hill 204, just west of Château-Thierry. The end of the Lys Offensive did not mean the end of German offensive action, as they would mount two more great offensives in the coming weeks.

"They Fell by the Scores"

On June 4 at 8:00 A.M., General Omar Bundy officially took charge of the American sector along the Western Front. The 23d Infantry now defended the line from the Paris-Metz road north to Triangle Farm. Major Thomas Holcomb's 2d Battalion, 6th Marines, then continued the line to Lucy, with Major Benjamin S. Berry's 3d Battalion, 5th Marines, extending to Hill 142. A steady flow of American artillery, communications, and supplies continued to move up, until the entire 2d Division stood in place by day's end.

General Omar Bundy (left) watches training maneuvers in France at the beginning of the war. He would take charge of the American sector on the Western Front.

Two days of standoff followed. Marine sharpshooters turned back several local assaults by the Germans. The Germans, advancing unwaveringly into the almost certain death of expert rifle fire, showed great courage and earned the marines' respect. A young private in Holcomb's 2d Battalion, 6th Marines, described one such assault:

The German barrage lifted; the French guns almost ceased firing. The men about me were cursing and swearing in that choice collection of profanity that belongs to the Marines. It took me back swiftly, on the wings of memory, to a lonely walk in the woods I had taken, as a boy, when I had whistled to keep up my courage.

The German troops were clear of the woods. On they came with closed ranks in four lines. One looked at them with almost a friendly interest. No particular hate or fear. And yet there was a queer sensation along the spine, and the scalp seemed to itch from the tug of hair at the roots. The fingers bit into the rifle.

"Hold your fire!"

As the command rang in my ears with the sharpness that enforced obedience, I seemed to be standing on Bunker Hill and hear the command: "Wait till you see the whites of their eyes!" I think I know how those old Yanks felt that day [during the Revolutionary War], as the enemy drew nearer and nearer.

The next I recall is firing. Firing. Firing. My fingers were tearing greedily at more ammunition, then the instinct of the hunter sustained me. I began to fire slower, looking for my mark, making sure they hit. The Huns [slang for Germans] now appeared to be almost on top of us and then, all of a sudden, there was nothing more to aim at. A few scattered groups with hands held up, racing for our lines and shouting "Kamerad! Kamerad!" ["Comrade!"]

Respect for their enemy did not deter the marines from chopping down a lot more Germans with their unerring marksmanship. Farther to the left, a member of Major Maurice Shearer's 1st Battalion, 6th Marines, recalled another German assault:

They came out of the wood opposite our position in close formation. They came on as steadily as if they were on parade. We opened up on them with a slashing barrage of rifles, automatics and machine guns. They were brave men— we had to grant them that. They had a good artillery barrage in front of them, but it didn't keep us down. Three times they tried to break through, but our fire was too heavy and too accurate for them. It was terrible in its effectiveness. They fell by the scores, there among the poppies and the wheat. Then they broke and ran for cover.

Except for such intermittent attempts by the Germans to breach the marine defenses, the two forces remained in place during June 4–5, separated by rifle and machine-gun fire and shrapnel showers.

On June 5, the right flank of Corps Conta failed to make even minimal advances and then was struck by counterattacking French poilus. A frustrated von Conta postponed his offensive and ordered his troops to dig in along their presently held line.

Work for the Marines

General Bundy used the temporary standstill to consolidate his positions. The French 167th Division arrived to bear a hand on his extreme left. With the 3d Brigade now in the south and the 4th Marine Brigade in the north, Bundy's two brigades touched at Triangle Farm. Each of his infantry and marine regiments, four in all, held some two thousand yards of line. All four regiments stood in with two battalions up and one in reserve.

On June 5, Colonel Preston Brown, General Bundy's chief of staff, telephoned General Harbord and summoned him to 2d Division headquarters. "We have work for your marines," Brown said.

A machine-gun crew takes advantage of a crater made by an artillery shell to set up their machine gun and fire on the enemy.

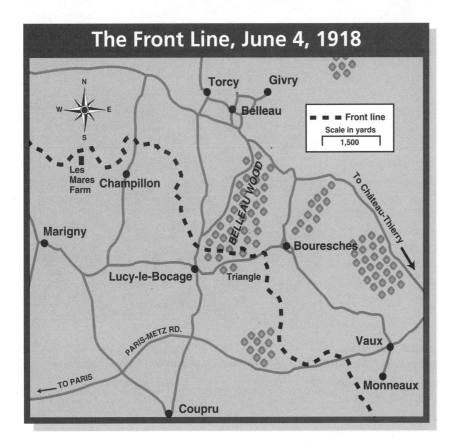

The Front Line, June 4, 1918

Torcy

Givry

Belleau

Front line

Scale in yards

1,500

Les Mares Farm

Champillon

BELLEAU WOOD

To Château-Thierry

Marigny

Bouresches

Lucy-le-Bocage

Triangle

PARIS-METZ RD.

Vaux

TO PARIS

Monneaux

Coupru

When Harbord arrived at division headquarters, in the town hall of Montreuil-aux-Lions, Colonel Brown briefed the 4th Marine Brigade commander on the tactical situation. General Degoutte, in overall charge of Allied operations in the 2d Division sector, had issued orders to counterattack before the Germans could firm up their gains and resume the advance. To kick off the Allied counterattack, Degoutte named the French 167th Division to move out at 3:45 the next morning (June 6) and secure the high ground south of the Clignon Brook. At the same time, Major Julius Turrill's 1st Battalion, 5th Marines, would assault Hill 142 to eliminate German flanking fire on the 167th.

A second, decisive phase of the operation was scheduled to commence later in the afternoon of June 6 at 5:00 P.M. If all went as planned, the 2d Division would then seize the ridge overlooking the villages of Torcy and Belleau, while at the same time occupying Belleau Wood and the town of Bouresches. But all would not go as planned.

A Costly Error

Earlier, on June 4, French troops moving to the rear through marine lines had informed the marines that Belleau Wood was clear of Germans. The marines then committed a costly error—an

Shoot-Out at Les Mares Farm

The marines showed their aggressive spirit and willingness to fight as soon as they arrived at the front on June 2, 1918. With 51st Company to its right, Captain John Blanchfield's 55th Company occupied a woods west of the village of Champillon. The woods stood in the center of the line held by the 2d Battalion, 5th Marines. Blanchfield and his marines watched from the woods as retreating French soldiers engaged the Germans in a deadly game of leapfrog, firing and falling back from cover to cover. Soon the French soldiers informed the marines that they had completed their withdrawal. Only Germans remained in front of the marines.

Blanchfield ordered his marines forward to establish a position in a cluster of buildings called Les Mares ("the ponds") Farm. The marines dug in and spent all night and the next morning under a heavy barrage of German artillery. After a brief lull, the Germans attacked Les Mares Farm in force on June 4.

The Germans advanced no closer than one hundred yards to the greatly outnumbered defenders. Positioned in buildings, wagons, haystacks, and behind a stone wall that surrounded the farm, the marines cut down their enemies with accurate rifle fire. Targeting the Germans and firing as if on rifle range, the marine sharpshooters withstood the German assault. After three waves of attackers failed to penetrate the marine defenses, the Germans withdrew and waited until the next day to try again.

American artillery pounded the German positions on June 5, but a few small groups of Germans attempted to advance on Les Mares Farm, using the adjacent wheat field for cover. Shortly before noon, Corporal Francis J. Dockx crawled back from an outpost thirty yards forward of the farm to report a suspicious movement of the wheat to his front. Gunnery Sergeant David Buford and a squad of marines

Soldiers of the 2d Battalion, 5th Marines, pose in front of a German trench mortar that they have just captured.

snaked their way back through the wheat to investigate. They discovered a group of thirty Germans with two machine guns trying to set up a machine-gun nest.

Buford and two of his men charged the surprised Germans, while the remainder of Buford's squad laid down covering fire. Most of the Germans tried to run. Marine snipers firing from rear haystacks helped to hasten their flight. Buford, a veteran marine and crack pistol shot, outflanked the fleeing Germans. Firing his .45 from a classic crouched position, he killed several Germans before rejoining his squad for an attack on the machine-gun crews.

Corporal Dockx and another marine were killed while rushing the machine guns. Of the thirty Germans, five made it back to their lines. The rest were either killed or captured.

In the shoot-out at Les Mares Farm, 55th Company had served notice to the Germans and to the world that the marines had come to fight.

General James G. Harbord poses with members of his staff. Standing from left to right are Major Harry Lay, Lieutenant Robinson, Major Smith, Lieutenant Williams, and Le Gasse.

error of omission—by not sending out reconnaissance patrols to see for themselves. General Harbord later attributed the marines' failure to patrol the wood to inexperience:

> The French had informed us that Belleau Wood was not occupied except by a very short line across the northeast corner which was entrenched. Little or no reconnaissance or scouting appears to have been done by the companies in front of their positions between June 4th and 6th, the responsibility having been ours since the withdrawal of the French on the 4th. This was probably due to inexperience. Maps were scarce, almost unobtainable, and the *hachures* [short lines used for shading and denoting surfaces in relief and drawn in the direction of slope] gave no real information as to the physical features of the ground. The Bois proved to be very fully occupied, with many machine-gun nests, in positions well chosen among the giant boulders.

> It is now established that the Germans had three lines of trenches in the wood—the first a little behind the southern edge facing toward Lucy and Bouresches; the second across the Wood from east to west at about the center from north to south; and the third about one hundred and fifty yards from the north end of the Wood just south of the old *pavillon* [pavilion] and the slope down to where the Cemetery is now

The Value of Belleau Wood

Major General Jean M. J. Degoutte, commander of the French XXI Corps and Allied operations in the American sector, believed that wars are won by offensive action. Until the arrival on-line of the U.S. 2d and 3d Divisions, Degoutte had been fighting a desperate defensive battle, his corps greatly outnumbered by the Germans and in imminent danger of collapse. With two fresh American divisions at his disposal, the French commander knew just what to do with them: *attack!*

At Degoutte's command, the 3d Division counterattacked at Château-Thierry, and the 2d Division's 4th Marine Brigade struck out boldly at Belleau Wood. Degoutte obviously recognized the value of Belleau Wood, as did the Germans; and, perhaps more so than anyone, the Americans. The 2d Division's commander, Major General Omar Bundy, felt that a German presence in the wood posed an ongoing threat to the American line:

The Germans had been prompt to see its value [Belleau Wood] as a place of conceal-ment for the assembly of infantry and machine guns to continue their attack. They had occupied it immediately with a regiment of infantry and numerous machine guns and trench mortars. It had the protection of their artillery, placed in concealed positions to the north. As long as they held it, it would be an ever-present menace to our line. A successful attack launched from it would force us off the Paris road, our main source of supply, and compel us to fight with our backs to the Marne, with probably disastrous results.

General Degoutte . . . saw the importance of Belleau Wood, and was in full accord with our desire to take it as soon as possible.

Commencing at 3:45 A.M. on June 6, 1918, "as soon as possible" turned out to be two and a half weeks of the fiercest fighting in warfare's bloody history. The battle for Belleau Wood would not end until 5 P.M. on June 24, 1918. Things of value often do not come easy.

located. Lines of barbed wire and sharpshooter rifle pits completed the system, the ruins of which are still seen by visiting tourists.

General Harbord wrote the foregoing description of German defenses years after the battle for Belleau Wood. Information about German preparedness *before* the battle, however, was both inaccurate and conflicting. Prior to the battle, General Degoutte's intelligence officer informed General Harbord that American troops would have to cross wide expanses of wheat fields when attacking the northern and central sections of Belleau Wood. "But you should not have any trouble capturing it," the French officer said. "It is lightly held by a very short line across the northeast corner." In reality, Belleau Wood was one enormous machine-gun nest.

Mystery of Belleau Wood

On the evening of June 5, the marines began to edge closer to the brink of chance destiny. As further evidence of the conflicting intelligence information that surrounded Belleau Wood, 6th Marine Regiment commander Catlin would later write:

> We now stood facing the dark, sullen mystery of Belleau Wood. . . . That the wood was strongly held we knew, and so we waited. . . . That something was going on within those threatening woods we knew, for our intelligence men were not idle. . . . The report on this morning [June 6] was to the effect that the Germans were organizing in the woods and were consolidating their machine gun positions, so that a sortie [attack] in force seemed not unlikely.

Now, only hours separated the marines from learning up close about the mystery within Belleau Wood.

A hastily dug trench shows the very primitive cover that soldiers constructed to protect themselves in Belleau Wood.

☆ ☆ ☆ ☆ ☆ ☆ ☆ ☆ ☆ ☆ ☆ ☆ ☆

CHAPTER FOUR

Hill 142

Major Julius Turrill was chosen to lead the assault on Hill 142.

The first phase of General Harbord's attack plan called for Major Julius Turrill's 1st Battalion, 5th Marines, to assault Hill 142 before dawn, aided by the 8th and 23d Machine Gun Companies and D Company of the 2d Engineers. Harbord's attack order, which had been issued at 10:25 P.M. on June 5, directed Turrill and his support groups to attack "between the brook of Champillon, inclusive, Hill 142, and the brook which flows from one kilometer [five-eighths of a mile] northeast of Champillon, inclusive."

Major Benjamin Berry's 3d Battalion, 5th Marines, was to press forward on Turrill's right and "conform to the progress made by the 1st Battalion in its attack." Once the two battalions had reached their objectives—a line on the far side of Hill 142—they were to consolidate and prepare for an enemy counterattack.

But as H-Hour drew near on June 6, most of Turrill's 1st Battalion, 5th Marines, were still scattered about on earlier assignments and out of position. Only Captain George W. Hamilton's 49th Company and Captain Orlando C. Crowther's 67th Company stood in place and ready to attack. Turrill's 17th and 66th Companies and the 8th Machine Gun Company were still on-line at Les Mares Farm, where they had been awaiting relief by French forces since 9 o'clock the previous night. Nor was there yet any sign of either the 23d Machine Gun Company or D Company of the 2d Engineers.

"Blue and Cool"

At H-5 (H-Hour minus five hours, or approximately 10:45 P.M., June 5), a combined American-French artillery group of six batteries of 75s and two of 155s opened fire. Their fire concentrated on targets around—rather than directly on—assigned objectives "so as not to attract the attention of the enemy." At the same time, this fire—called interdiction and raking fire—was meant to sever the enemy's lines of supply and communication and thus isolate the intended objectives.

The French 167th Division, on the marines' left, attacked on schedule in the early morning darkness of June 6. The poilus advanced easily at first and overran several German entrenchments. Then the French artillery failed to lengthen the range fast enough to stay ahead of the advancing troops. Their own shells began to pound the French infantrymen and inflicted heavy casualties. Confused, shaken, and caught in a crossfire of French and German artillery, the poilus quickly returned to their line of departure.

To the right of the 167th, moments before H-Hour, Turrill was still not ready to attack. None of his missing companies had arrived. Crowther's 67th Company had not made contact with the French on the left, nor had Hamilton's 49th Company tied with Berry's 3d Battalion on the right. Turrill would have to make do with a skeleton crew.

The marines of both companies spread out along an eight-hundred-yard front just northwest of Belleau Wood. Stripped of all unnecessary gear, they wore twenty-pound combat packs and carried hand grenades, bandoliers of extra ammunition, and gas masks. A wheat field separated the marines from their objectives: Hill 142—a low, pine-covered mound—about a thousand yards to the northeast; and beyond the hill, a section of road between Torcy and Lucy-le-Bocage.

At precisely 3:45 A.M., after a brief artillery and machine-gun barrage directly on their objectives, Crowther and Hamilton blew their whistles. And two companies of marines rose up as one from shallow trenches and launched their attack in four waves, plunging into the wheat fields with bayonets fixed.

Captain John W. Thomason Jr., a machine-gun officer with the 5th Marines and a writer who has been called the "Kipling of the Corps," wrote:

> The platoons came out of the woods as dawn was getting gray. The light was strong when they advanced into the open wheat, now all starred with poppies, red as blood. To the east the sun appeared, immensely red and round, a handbreadth above the horizon; a German shell burst black across the face of it, just to the left of the line. Men turned their heads to see, and many there looked no more upon the sun forever. . . . It was a beautiful deployment, lines all dressed and guiding true. Such matters were of deep concern to this outfit. The day was without a cloud, promising heat later, but now it was pleasant in the wheat, and the woods around looked blue and cool.

Two Hard-Pressed Companies

Accounts of great events often vary greatly as influenced by the vantage point and bias of the viewer. Lieutenant Colonel Ernst Otto, a German army officer, recounted the first French and American attacks on June 6 with a German slant:

In accordance with orders from General Degoutte, at 4:45 A.M. the 1st and 2nd Battalions of the 5th Marines joined the French 167th Division in the attack, the 1st Battalion on the left, the 2nd on the right. This attack struck the 460th Regiment, and the 9th Company of the 462nd Regiment, echeloned [stepped] to the right. As the French had succeeded in making a temporary entry into Bussiares . . . the 9th Company of the 462nd Regiment, and the 9th Company of the 460th Regiment, were surrounded by superior forces and cut off in the early morning hours, and, after a particularly brave defense, were practically annihilated. Only a small number of the 9th Company, 460th Regiment, succeeded in fighting their way back to their battalion with their bayonets. The 10th and 11th Companies, 460th, dug themselves in, in their patch of woods southwest of Torcy, in the face of the enemy attacking on all sides. They repulsed the attacks with severe losses, but were continually harassed by low fliers who almost touched the tree tops. The few available reserves were rushed in turn to the places where the enemy was approaching the closest, sometimes within a few paces. A vigorous counterattack by the 12th company, whose company commander fell in this comradely endeavor, cleared the way to the north. The enemy now covered the woods with heavy artillery fire, including gas shells. To have sent further support would have entailed severe losses; the regimental commander, Lieutenant Colonel Tismer, therefore decided to withdraw both companies. Of course, this could only be done after dark. Accordingly, these two hard-pressed companies withstood the enemy attacks most creditably during the whole day.

The "blue and cool" turned quickly to red and hot. And the heat came not from the sun. After advancing some fifty yards, German machine guns cut loose and began chopping the marines to pieces.

"Too Many Guns"

The tactic of advancing in four neatly aligned waves had been developed by the French and Germans for traversing the short distances between the trenches of no-man's-land. Theoretically, three waves might fall in an attack on the enemy's trenches, but the fourth would survive to gain the objective. This concept of crazy calculus cost the lives of more than ten million soldiers in World War I. The marines, in the early going, paid a high price for using this tactic. They never used the method again. "It was," as Captain Thomason noted, "unadapted for open warfare."

The German Maxim machine guns might have ended the marine attack in the first few minutes except for the courage and leadership of Captain George Hamilton. Turrill's battalion adjutant, Captain Keller Rockey, described Hamilton as "well qualified professionally, sound, brave, a fine leader respected by his men, his [peers] and his seniors." A well-built, athletic young man, Hamilton rallied a few survivors and waved them toward a small woods. He later described the attack in a letter to a friend:

> I realized that we were up against something unusual and had to run along the whole line and get each man (almost individually) on his feet to rush that wood. Once inside, things went better, but from here on I don't remember clearly what happened.

Things went better inside because those marines who survived the hail of machine-gun fire rushed headlong into the dark and fought the entrenched enemy at close quarters with steel, skewering every German in their path. A handful of Germans surrendered in time to avoid a brutal death at the end of a bayonet. Most did not.

While Hamilton's men were rooting out the enemy with sixteen inches of steel, Crowther's 67th Company swept by to the left of the wood. A group of Maxims, concealed by a thicket off a flanking ravine, started chattering in unison and halted Crowther's advancing troops. Captain Crowther and First Sergeant

Captain George Hamilton roused his troops to brave German machine-gun fire and attack the Germans in hand-to-hand combat.

This illustration depicts German and American troops facing off in the type of brutal hand-to-hand combat that eventually won the war for the Allies.

The American Regular

Captain John W. Thomason Jr., a career marine officer and talented writer, described marines at war as have few writers, past or present. Of the assault on Hill 142, Thomason wrote:

> Platoons were formed in four waves, the attack formation taught by the French, a formation proved in trench warfare, where there was a short way to go, and you calculated on losing the first three waves and getting the fourth one to the objective. The Marines never used it again. It was a formation unadapted for open warfare, and incredibly vulnerable. It didn't take long to learn better, but there was a price to pay for the learning.

That price was paid by the 49th and 67th Companies of the 5th Marines. Just before dawn on June 6, 1918, the two companies formed up in four lines and entered the wheat field in front of Hill 142. Thomason continued:

> Pretty country, those rolling wheatlands northwest of Château-Thierry, with copses [clumps] of trees and little tidy forests where French sportsmen maintained hunting-lodges and game-preserves. Since the first Marne [in 1914] there had been no war here. The [marine] files found it very different from the mangled red terrain around Verdun, and much nicer to look at. "Those poppies, now. Right pretty, ain't they?"—a tall corporal picked one and stuck it in his helmet buckle, where it blazed against his leathery cheek. There was some shelling—not much, for few of the German guns had caught up, the French had lost all theirs, and the American artillery was still arriving.
>
> Across this wheat-field there were more woods, and in the edge of these woods the old Boche, lots of him, infantry and machine-guns. Surely he had seen the platoons forming a few hundred yards away—it is possible that he did not believe his eyes. He let them come close before he opened fire. The American fighting man has his failings. He is prone to many regrettable errors. But the [wise] enemy will never let him get close enough to see whom he is attacking. When he has seen the enemy, the American regular will come on in. To stop him you must kill him. And when he is properly trained and has somebody to say "Come on!" to him, he will stand as much killing as anybody on earth.

Daniel A. Hunter went down at once—both dead when they hit the ground. Hamilton, also under heavy fire, continued to direct his decimated platoons through the woods.

> I have vague recollections of urging the whole line on, faster, perhaps, than they should have gone—of grouping prisoners and sending them to the rear under *one* man instead of several—of snatching an Iron Cross ribbon off the first officer I got—and of shooting wildly at several rapidly retreating Boches. (I carried a rifle on the whole trip and used it to good advantage.) Farther on, we came to an open field—a wheat field full of red poppies—and here we caught hell.

The Maxims continued to fire, *chigga-chigging* flying metal at their full rate of five hundred rounds a minute, sweeping low to the ground across interlocking fields of fire. The low-flying projectiles nearly sliced the combat packs off the backs of some marines—the more fortunate ones—even though they lay flattened on the ground. They pressed ahead in desperation and soon emerged in another open wheat field. More savage fire raked across their front. Hamilton waved his troops on toward another small woods.

> Again it was a case of rushing across the open and getting into the woods. Afterwards we found why it was they made it so hot for us—three *machine-gun companie*s were holding down these woods and the infantry were farther back. Besides several of the heavy Maxims we later found several empty belts and a dead gunner sitting on the seat or lying near by. It was only because we rushed the positions that we were able to take them, as there were too many guns to take them in any other way.

In their rush to seize the enemy positions, Hamilton's men overran their objective by at least six hundred yards.

"All My Officers Are Gone"

Possibly the poor quality of the maps furnished for marine use had contributed more than a little to Hamilton's failure to recog-

Many marines died while trying to rout the Germans from machine-gun nests such as these. Once entrenched, the Germans mowed down the advancing American and French troops.

nize his objective. The only available maps of the locale had been drawn to a very small scale by the French Dépôt de la Guerre (War Depot) in 1832 and updated in 1912. Since 1832, whole forests had grown and many roads had been built. Some had been added to the old maps and some had not, as Hamilton later indicated:

> After going through this second wood we were really at our objective, but I was looking for an unimproved road which showed up on the map. We now had the Germans pretty well on the run except a few machine-gun nests. I was anxious to get to the road, so pushed forward with the men I had with me—one platoon (I knew the rest were coming, but thought they were closer). We went right down over the nose of a hill and on across an open field between two hills. What saved me from getting hit I don't know—the Maxims on both sides cut at us unmercifully—but although I lost heavily here I came out unscratched. I was pushing ahead with an automatic rifle team and didn't notice that most of the platoon had swerved to the left to rout the machine guns. All I knew was that there was a road ahead and that the bank gave good protection *to the front.*

Three of Hamilton's marines made it to Torcy. One of them, wounded, returned to the marine lines for help. The remaining two took shelter in a hole and continued to fight. Two enemy soldiers charged the hole. All four men died there.

At this point, Hamilton had lost all five of his junior officers, while one officer of five had survived in Crowther's 67th Company. Then it became clear to Hamilton that he had missed his objective:

> I realized that I had gone too far—that the nose of the hill I had come over was our objective, and that it was up to me to get back, reorganize, and dig in. It was a case of every man for himself. I crawled back through a drainage ditch filled with cold water and shiny reeds. Machine-gun bullets were just grazing my back and our own artillery was dropping close (I was six hundred yards too far to the front). Finally I got back, and started getting the two companies together.

Hamilton somehow managed to regroup the scattered marines from both companies, establishing strong points and setting up a defensive line just in time to repel a series of counterattacks by battalions of the German 197th and 237th Divisions. The Germans challenged Hamilton's makeshift defenses at once, hurling grenades at the few remaining marines. Hamilton dispatched a dire message to Major Turrill:

> Elements of this Company and the 67th Company reached their objective, but because very much disorganized were

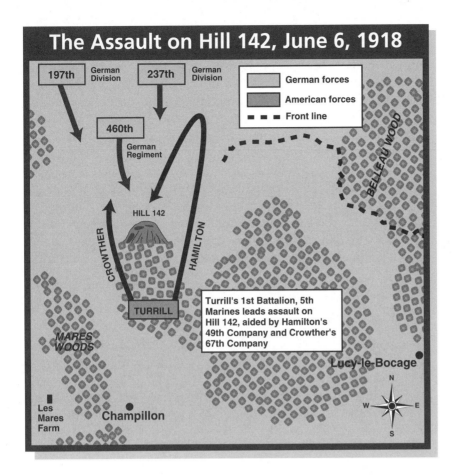

The Assault on Hill 142, June 6, 1918

197th — German Division
237th — German Division
460th — German Regiment

German forces
American forces
Front line

HILL 142

CROWTHER

HAMILTON

TURRILL

MARES WOODS

BELLEAU WOOD

Turrill's 1st Battalion, 5th Marines leads assault on Hill 142, aided by Hamilton's 49th Company and Crowther's 67th Company

Lucy-le-Bocage

Les Mares Farm

Champillon

N S E W

forced to retire to our present position which is on the nose of Hill 142 and about 400 yards northeast of square woods. . . . Our position is not good because of salient. We are intrenching and have 4 machine guns in place. . . .

We have been counter-attacked several times but so far have held this hill. Our casualties are *very* heavy. We need medical aid badly, cannot locate any hospital apprentices and need many. We will need artillery assistance to hold this line tonight.

Ammunition of all kinds is needed.

The line is being held by detachments from the 49th, 66th and 67th Compan[ies] and are very much mixed together.

No Very pistols. All my officers are gone.

"On Our Objective"

Forty-ninth Company's Gunnery Sergeant Ernest A. Janson spotted a dozen Germans with automatic weapons crawling toward the marine positions. Janson shouted a warning, charged the

Sergeant Ernest A. Janson's quick thinking kept the marines' 67th Company from being wiped out by advancing Germans.

Germans, and plunged his bayonet into the first two. Other marines came running to Janson's aid and drove off the remaining Germans, who had been attempting to set up five machine guns on the marines' flank. If not for Janson's alertness and courageous reaction, 67th Company would surely have been wiped out. For his selfless act in saving his comrades, Janson became the first marine to earn the Medal of Honor in World War I.

By then, the rest of Turrill's 1st Battalion had started showing up. Each unit was pressed into action upon its arrival. Captain Lloyd Williams's 51st Company, of Wise's 2d Battalion, filled a void on Turrill's left. Still, Turrill's right flank, as well as his left flank beyond 51st Company, remained open and unprotected. At 1:10 P.M., Turrill notified his regimental commander, Colonel Wendell Neville, of 1st Battalion's situation:

> Our first line is on our objective—left weak—right uncovered. Think French are slowly advancing on our left. . . . A strong attack on our right would finish us.

That attack never came. The German 197th Division reported two thousand casualties from June 4 to June 6 and was forced to seek replacements.

The first phase of the June 6 fighting had cost Turrill's battalion nine officers and most of its 325 men. But the marines now owned Hill 142.

☆ ☆ ☆ ☆ ☆ ☆ ☆ ☆ ☆ ☆ ☆ ☆ ☆

CHAPTER FIVE

Foothold in the Forest

The critical second phase of the American offensive kicked off at 5:00 P.M. on June 6. About three hours of daylight remained when Berry's 3d Battalion, 5th Marines, and Sibley's 3d Battalion, 6th Marines, climbed over the top of their shallow trenches and entered the fields of waist-high wheat. Berry attacked Belleau Wood from the west; Sibley struck toward the wood's southwestern hook.

Slipping the Leash

Since this was supposed to have been a surprise attack, no artillery barrage had preceded the marine assault, according to the 4th Marine Brigade commander, General James G. Harbord.

> With the information that we had had [from the French] that the woods were unoccupied by the Germans, we gave it no artillery preparation, thinking thereby to take it by surprise or to find it unoccupied.

General Harbord's recollection contradicted an entry in the 4th Brigade's War Diary for June 6 at 5:00 P.M.:

> Artillery starting with raking fire on Bois de Belleau and on the northern and eastern slopes, 2nd interdiction fire on the ravine, railroad, and road between Bouresches and Belleau-Torcy-Lucy-Clignon and Bussiares, with the 75s.

With regard to a German presence in Belleau Wood, Harbord's words also stood at odds with those of Colonel Albertus C.

Major Benjamin Berry attacked Belleau Wood from the west during the second phase of the Battle of Belleau Wood.

Bois de Belleau

"The Bois de Belleau," wrote General James G. Harbord, "was an irregular area of perhaps a square mile of timbered land, once a hunting preserve for the ancient Château of Belleau, which with its village was about half a mile north of the Wood." Harbord, the commander of the 4th Marine Brigade, continued:

> Lucy lay just west of the southern end of the Wood. Bouresches was a small village at the southeast corner of it. From Lucy to the old Château of Belleau there ran a farm road. From Torcy and Belleau a fairly important road and a railroad ran past the eastern edge of the Wood through Bouresches and on to Château-Thierry, perhaps five miles distant. A deep ravine, dry at that season, skirted the southern edge of the Wood, crossing a road which led from Lucy to the Paris-Metz highway. . . . A road from Lucy to Bouresches paralleled this ravine along the southern end of the Wood. . . . The timber was what in this country would be called second growth, but it had never been underbrushed and there was a dense tangle of undergrowth, with here and there a wood road through it. Some small areas had been cut off and the cordwood was piled in the clearings. The topography of the greater part of the Wood, especially in the eastern and southern portions, was extremely rugged and rocky, none of which was shown in maps available at the time. Great irregular boulders, from the size of a small freight car to that of a small motor-car, were piled up and over and against one another by some prehistoric convulsion. These afforded shelter for machine-gun nests, with disposition in depth and flanking one another, generally so rugged that only direct hits of artillery were effective against them. The Wood afforded concealment for infantry, and was what is technically known in the Army as a strong point. It stood at the extreme southwest angle of the salient which the enemy had created by his advance from the Aisne [River], and was at its closest point to Paris. Occupied by our troops, it barred the further advance of Germans on the Paris-Metz highway. It was insignificant in area, not especially picturesque, out of the ordinary track of travel and with no particular traditions of peace or of earlier wars. The accident of place and the chance stroke of zero hour wrote the name of the Bois de Belleau on the records.

Catlin, the commander of the 6th Marines, who later wrote:

> On the night of the 4th Lieutenant Eddy, the intelligence officer of the Sixth [Marine Regiment], with two men stole through the German lines and penetrated the enemy country almost as far as Torcy. They lay in a clover field near the road and watched the Germans filing past them. They listened to the talk and observed what was going on in the woods.

Scant as this information was, it offered clear evidence that the Germans did, indeed, occupy Belleau Wood.

In the midst of such confusion, it seems clearer yet that Harbord's brigade was no more ready for the late-afternoon attack on Belleau Wood than it had been for the early morning assault on Hill 142. Catlin, in fact, had not received written brigade orders informing him of overall command responsibility for the attack until about 3:00 P.M.—two hours before H-Hour. Catlin took the orders with more than a few misgivings:

> I was supposed to direct Berry's movements, though he had also received the orders from his own [5th] regimental headquarters. I telephoned at once to Berry's P.C. [post of command] at Lucy, but his battalion was beyond reach and he was himself in the woods in their rear, a mile away. It had been impossible, on account of the heavy shelling, to run a telephone out to him. I sent runners, but I was sure they couldn't reach him before the attack would have to be made.

> I must confess that this situation caused me considerable anxiety. I don't know whose fault it was, but the communications were far from perfect. It looked as though we would have to attack without proper coordination.

Colonel Catlin briefed his 6th battalion commanders quickly then hurried off toward Lucy to observe the action. He found Sibley's 3d Battalion, 6th Marines, along the way,

> waiting in the sheltered trenches, ready to go over the top. They were equipped for action. When Marines go into the line they travel in heavy marching order, but when they go into a fight it is in light marching order, with no extra clothing or any blankets. They carry 20-odd pounds then. They all had their rifle and ammunition and some of the men were equipped with hand or rifle grenades. The machine guns were in position . . . just back of the front line. Each company had eight automatic rifles and eight in reserve. . . . The men seemed cool, in good spirits, and ready for the word to start. They were talking quietly among themselves. I spoke to several as I passed. . . .

> On my left I passed some of Berry's men, the right end of the battalion. They too seemed to be ready and waiting for the leash to be slipped.

When the leash slipped at 5:00 P.M. and the marines plunged into the wheat fields, the Germans in the wood were expecting them.

Across the Field and into the Wood

Massed German Maxims rippled the wheat fields with interlocking bands of machine-gun fire and chopped huge gaps in the ranks of the exposed marines. The vicious fire forced the marines to scratch ground on their bellies.

(Top) Gunnery Sergeant Dan Daly tried to hustle the marines into action when whole groups of them perished under vicious German machine-gun fire. Sadly, the German fire did not lessen and many more marines died while following Daly's command. (Bottom) A ruined home near Belleau Wood gives evidence of the heavy fire the area received during the battle.

Then a voice rang out above the *chigga-chig-chigging* of the Maxims: "Come on, you sons-o'-bitches! Do you want to live forever?" It was the voice of veteran Gunnery Sergeant Dan Daly, of the 73d Marine Machine Gun Company, urging his men forward.

The marines again advanced in their well-disciplined—but sadly inefficient—lines and were mowed down in their tracks. The withering German fire took a fierce toll. Major Berry was severely wounded in the left forearm during the advance. Floyd Gibbons, a renowned war correspondent for the *Chicago Tribune* rushed to aid Berry and was himself struck by three machine-gun slugs.

Gibbons and Lieutenant Oscar Hartzell, one of General Pershing's press officers and a former journalist for the *New York Times*, had arrived at Colonel Neville's post of command in La Voie du Châtel a little before four o'clock that afternoon. Gibbons informed Neville that he and Hartzell intended to proceed immediately to the front. "Go wherever you like," Neville replied. "Go as far as you like, but I want to tell you it's damn hot up there." The two reporters set out for Berry's position.

"An hour later found us in the woods to the west of Lucy le Bocage," Gibbons would write later.

To the west and north another nameless cluster of farm dwellings was in flames. Huge clouds of smoke rolled up like a smudge against the background of blue sky. . . .

Occasional shells were dropping in the woods, which were also within range from a long distance [of] indirect machine gun fire from the enemy. Bits of lead, wobbling in their flight at the end of their long trajectory, sung through the air above our heads and clipped leaves and twigs from the branches.

"Attacking with Tenacity"

At 6:50 P.M. on June 6, 1918, less than two hours after the marines had launched the second phase of their attack on Belleau Wood, Major General von Diepenbroick-Grüter, the commander of the German 10th Division, issued an order stating: "We must expect continuous attacks on the front of the 10th Division."

Accordingly, Lieutenant Colonel Ernst Otto, a German army officer and battle analyst, later wrote:

> The attack of the 3rd Battalion, 5th Marines, and the 2nd and 3rd Battalions, 6th Marines, late that evening, was therefore not unexpected by the Germans. It was directed chiefly against the left wing of the 398th Regiment, particularly the 1st Battalion, and the right wing of the 47th Regiment, the 1st Battalion. The Americans were obliged to come down from the heights they were occupying before the eyes of the Germans. They did this in thick lines of skirmishers, supported by columns following immediately behind. The Germans could not have desired better targets; such a spectacle was entirely unfamiliar to them. Under similar conditions, German troops would have advanced in thin lines of skirmishers following one another like waves, or in small, separate units of shock troops, moving forward in rows with their light machine guns, utilizing whatever shelter was offered by the terrain until they were in a position to open fire. It was thus that the French had advanced the same day, through the grain fields, until they had crept close to the German defenders. However, when one considers that this was their first real fight this procedure of the Americans is by no means surprising. Troops coming under fire for the first time often proceed in just that way. The German soldiers of 1914, generally conceded to have constituted the best army ever known, often advanced in almost the same way as the Americans did on this occasion, despite orders to the contrary. This is evident from French and English descriptions of the early battles. And yet in those days they defeated all the French and English armies, driving them back of the Marne, although they suffered great losses, particularly in officers. It is, therefore, perfectly clear why the vigorous American battalions adopted that method of advancing to the attack. And it was only natural that the entire artillery, machine-gun, and infantry fire of the defenders should have been concentrated on these advancing masses. It was thus that the first attack broke down with severe losses.

This failure by no means disheartened the Americans. They kept on attacking with tenacity.

Part of the tenacious American forces that refused to give up until they defeated the Germans.

Gibbons barely had time to gulp down a can of "Corned Willy" before one of Berry's platoon leaders announced: "We are going forward in five minutes." Gibbons remembered:

> And then we went over. There are really no heroics about it. There is no bugle call, no sword waving, no dramatic enunciation of catchy commands, no theatricalism—it's just plain get up and go over. And it is done just the same as one would walk across a peaceful wheat field out in Iowa.

> But with the appearance of our first line, as it stepped from the shelter of the woods into the open exposure of the flat field, the woods opposite began to crackle and rattle with enemy machine gun fire. Our men advanced in open order, ten and twelve feet between men. Sometimes a squad would run forward fifty feet and drop. And as its members flattened on the ground for safety another squad would rise from the ground and make another rush.

> They gained the woods. Then we could hear shouting. Then we knew the work was being done with the bayonet. The machine gun fire continued in intensity and then died down completely. The wood had been won.

The Wounds of War

Gibbons and Hartzell then met up with Major Berry and a party of some fifteen marines at the edge of a clearing about two hundred yards wide. German machine guns occupied the opposite woods in force. "We could hear them," Gibbons recalled. "We could not see them but we knew that every leaf and piece of greenery there vibrated from their fire and the tops of the young oats waved and swayed with the streams of lead that swept across."

Then the woods sheltering Gibbons and the marines came under heavy machine-gun fire. Flat on their stomachs, with Major Berry in the lead, the men started across the open field to silence the enemy guns. Berry took a hit at once. Gibbons heard him cry out:

> "My hand's gone," he shouted. One of the streams of lead had found him. A ball had entered his left arm at the elbow, had travelled down the side of the bone, tearing away muscles and nerves of the forearm and lodging itself in the palm of his hand. His pain was excruciating.

Gibbons crawled to Berry's aid.

> And then it happened. The lighted end of a cigarette [a bullet] touched me in the fleshy part of my left arm. . . . Then the second one hit. It nicked the top of my left shoulder. . . .

And then the third one struck me. . . . I brought my right hand toward my face and placed it to the left of my nose. My fingers rested on something soft and wet. I withdrew my fingers and looked at it. It was covered with blood. As I looked at it, I was not aware that my entire vision was confined to my right eye, although there was considerable pain in the entire left side of my face. . . . I did not know then, as I know now, that a bullet striking the ground immediately under my left cheek bone, had ricochetted upward, going completely through the left eye and then crashing out through my forehead, leaving the eyeball and upper eyelid completely halved, the lower eyelid torn away, and a compound fracture of the skull.

Gibbons lost his left eye to the third bullet. Berry, despite his wound, got up and rushed forward to rejoin his men.

Journalist Floyd Gibbons, left, lost his eye while braving enemy fire to report on the Battle of Belleau Wood for the Chicago Tribune.

In their effort to advance through the woods, Major Berton W. Sibley's troops hurled grenades at the German lines and engaged in fierce hand-to-hand fighting. Most of his men made it into the woods.

Like Cavemen They Fought

Contrary to Gibbons's optimistic appraisal, the woods had not been won. A few of Berry's marines had reached the edge of the wood but could not hold their hard-won positions. After dark, following an action that General Harbord later described as "a costly failure, bravely attempted," the marines crawled back to their lines.

To Berry's right, Major Sibley's 3d Battalion, 6th Marines, experienced similar difficulties. Moving out in the disastrous four-wave formation, they swept in even, widely spaced lines across the fields of waist-high wheat, toward the southwestern hook of Belleau Wood. German Maxims, aimed low, started chattering immediately. Men fell, their legs chopped out from under them. A sniper's bullet caught Colonel Catlin as he watched his men advance. Colonel Harry Lee was rushed forward and assumed overall command of the marines at the front.

Most of Sibley's marines on his left side reached the wood. Captain Dwight Smith's 82d Company cleared out a few German outposts with rifles and bayonets, then penetrated several hundred yards into the wood. Enemy machine-gun fire raked the tangled underbrush. Scattered nests of Maxims were positioned so that each gun provided protective fire for another. Snipers and barbed-wire entanglements impeded the marines' progress. First Lieutenant Alfred H. Noble's 83d Company also drew heavy fire. Both companies became disoriented in the frenzied fighting and swerved their direction of advance from east to north.

Sibley himself led his marines forward in rushes. Keeping low and hurling grenades, the marines pushed relentlessly deeper into the forest. In riotous hand-to-hand fighting, they used rifle and bayonet to best advantage. The battle likened to an age of cavemen and clubs—man against man in a fight for survival.

With the Help of God and a Few Marines

Second Lieutenant Louis T. Timmerman, of 83d Company, led his platoon straight through the mile-wide wood. In a clearing on the far side of the wood, the platoon huddled by a mound of rocks and took fire from every direction. Timmerman immediately ordered his troops back inside the wood, where they proceeded to capture two German machine guns. Thinking he had cleared the wood of Germans, Timmerman again ventured outside the wood, this time to be torn up by a wicked concentration of enemy fire. Timmerman later recorded the action in his diary:

> I again advanced out to the mound. The machine gun fire from the town [Bouresches] opened up all around. I halted the platoon behind the mound.

Immediately a terrible fire from the left flank was opened up from a little rise of ground about 50 yards away, also from our left rear by machine guns. I faced around and saw [Private] Swenson lying dead with a bullet hole through his forehead. At the same time I shouted to "Open fire to the right" pointing toward the hillock where a terrific fire was coming from. At this moment we had only been at the mound a minute or so while all this happened. I was hit in the left side of the face and fell forward thinking, "I've got mine," as I thought a bullet had ripped through under my eye. It knocked me out for a minute and then I felt better and although I was covered with blood I realized I had not been dangerously hit. My men were dropping around there so I told them to follow me and we ran back for the shelter of the woods.

Timmerman regrouped his remaining six men and resumed fighting, turning the two captured machine guns back on the Germans. A few stray marines joined him. Then, a few more, until his group swelled to forty marines. With the help of God and these few marines, Timmerman fought on and held his ground. His determined efforts earned him the Distinguished Service Cross.

Battling at Bouresches

On Sibley's right side, murderous fire confronted Captain Randolph T. Zane's 79th Company, of Major Holcomb's 2d Battalion, 6th Marines. Lieutenant Graves B. Erskine's platoon alone lost fifty-three of fifty-eight men in forty minutes. Erskine—another future Marine commandant—sent a wounded marine to find Zane and report that his, Erskine's, platoon could not move forward. The runner returned to Erskine's position within the hour with Zane's answer: "Goddammit, continue the advance!" Erskine did.

Meanwhile, Holcomb's 96th Company, led by Captain Donald F. Duncan, assaulted the village of Bouresches at the southeast corner of the wood. Duncan calmly smoked a pipe while advancing on the town, then suddenly took a Maxim bullet in the gut. He was killed moments later by an artillery shell. Sergeant Al Sheridan witnessed Duncan's death and described it later in a letter home:

> [We] carried him to a small clump of trees, all the time he was gasping, hit through the stomach, we no more than laid him on the ground when a big 8 in. shell came in and killed all but myself, I was knocked down but my helmet saved me, so I left them and rejoined my platoon.

Lieutenant James F. Robertson then assumed command and said, "Come on, let's go." Thirty marines of 96th Company's 2d, 3d, and 4th Platoons formed a skirmish line behind Robertson and headed toward Bouresches.

Along the way, another round hit Second Lieutenant Clifton B. Cates, leader of the 4th Platoon and still another future marine commandant. In a later report, Cates wrote:

> When within about 200 yards of the town, I was struck on the helmet by a machine gun bullet which knocked me unconscious. I soon regained consciousness and saw Lieutenant Robertson with my platoon . . . entering the western part of town, and I saw a few men just in front who were firing upon the town with a Chauchot [Chauchat automatic rifle], and the Germans were running out, I took the four men who were left and went on into the center of town where Corporal Finn and Sergeant Earl F. Belfrey established a Chauchot [sic] post. All the Germans had gotten out with the exception of a few who occupied the northern edge. In a few minutes I saw Lieutenant Robertson with the men that he had leaving the town and going out across the wheat field to the rear. I yelled at him but he could not hear me, so I blew my platoon whistle and he came over and turned the men over to me, and told me to go in and establish posts and hold the town.

While Robertson went back for reinforcements, Cates and twenty-two marines held the town for thirty desperate minutes. Then help began to arrive from another platoon of 96th Company and the remnants of Captain Randolph T. Zane's 79th Company. The isolated marines secured the town and drove off a German counterattack. But their ammunition was then running dangerously low.

When word reached the 6th Marines' post of command that the marines in Bouresches needed ammunition, Second Lieutenant William B. Moore and regimental Sergeant Major John H. Quick volunteered to deliver a truckload. Together, they roared off in the dark, down a shell-pocked road zeroed in on by German artillery and machine-gun fire. Through shock and shell, they delivered the goods to the outskirts of the besieged village, for which they each later received both the Distinguished Service Cross and the Navy Cross.

Heavy Losses

The dark brought with it a nightmare of confusion along the battle line. Units were scattered here and there. Officers were unable to restore order and regain control of their disheveled units. Many disoriented marines fell victim to German artillery; many others, to friendly fire. The wounded lay where they had fallen. At 10:10 P.M., Colonel Harry Lee, the new commander of the 6th Marines, informed General Harbord:

> Sibley reports unable to advance infantry because of strong machine gun positions and artillery. He had heavy losses. Or-

After losing fifty-three of his fifty-eight men in forty minutes, Lieutenant Graves B. Erskine (pictured) told his commanding officer, Randolph Zane, that he could no longer move forward. But in the desperate struggle typical of Belleau Wood, Zane only replied, "Goddammit, continue the advance."

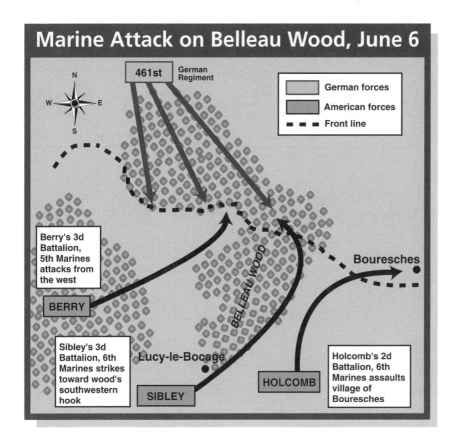

Marine Attack on Belleau Wood, June 6

461st — German Regiment

German forces
American forces
Front line

BERRY — Berry's 3d Battalion, 5th Marines attacks from the west

BELLEAU WOOD

Bouresches

Sibley's 3d Battalion, 6th Marines strikes toward wood's southwestern hook

SIBLEY

Lucy-le-Bocage

HOLCOMB — Holcomb's 2d Battalion, 6th Marines assaults village of Bouresches

dered him hold position at far edge Bois de Belleau, 47th Company, 3d Battalion, 5th Marines reorganizing at this point. Seems impossible to attack hostile gun positions without artillery. Request instructions.

Harbord responded to Lee's adjutant, Major Francis Evans:

Tell Colonel Lee two companies engineers coming up with tools. Use them to consolidate positions now attained. Make no further attempt to advance tonight. Give me report of conditions at daylight or before if you can form reliable information.

Two companies of the 2d Engineers slipped in during the night to reinforce marine positions. The number of Americans in Bouresches then totaled about seven hundred. Together, the marines and soldiers settled in for the night.

By morning, the 4th Marine Brigade had suffered casualties in the amount of 31 officers and 1,056 men. Among the casualties, 6 officers and 222 men were either killed or later died of wounds. But the marines now occupied Bouresches and had established a foothold in Belleau Wood.

CHAPTER SIX

Devil Dogs

Dawn broke on June 7 to reveal a battleground littered with dead and wounded. The marines now occupied a line more or less from Triangle Farm to Bouresches—although the Germans still held the railroad station there—through the bottom of Belleau Wood and then north to Hill 142. Shelling persisted all day long, keeping troops of both sides huddled in place.

Although the marines had just begun to fight, their first clashes had already captured world attention. Headlines in the June 7 edition of the *New York Times* proclaimed:

OUR TROOPS RESISTLESS. WHOLE DETACHMENTS OF GERMANS WIPED OUT. NO HOLDING BACK OUR MEN.

The *Times* might have overstated the marine advances somewhat, but such banners in newspapers across the country attracted long lines of eager young patriots at Marine Corps recruiting stations.

In such brief battle, the marines had also captured the admiration of their allies abroad. British prime minister Lloyd George commended the marines for their "superb valor and skill." Marshal Ferdinand Foch, France's greatest general and the supreme commander of Allied forces, issued an official communiqué lauding the marines: "They have won the admiration of the French troops with whom they fought."

Shortly after midnight on June 8, the Germans launched a counterattack, which the marines promptly repulsed. Major Berton W. Sibley's 3d Battalion, 6th Marines, struck back with an attack of their own at 4:00 A.M. The Germans reacted in kind, inflicting heavy losses on the marines and halting their advance by 10 A.M. The 461st Regiment, German 237th Division, later reported:

The town of Bouresches, completely destroyed during the Battle of Belleau Wood.

At 5:00 A.M. the enemy renewed his attack along the entire front of this regiment. Beaten back everywhere else, he succeeded in penetrating on the left wing, favored as he was by the possession of Bouresches. A counterattack by the 6th and 8th Companies, 461st, and the 365th Engineer Company, threw the Americans back to their original position in the woods. The mass of dead lying in front of the point where they temporarily broke our line indicates that the enemy suffered great losses. Forty prisoners were taken by the 461st Regiment.

Sibley's report to brigade headquarters echoed the German account of the marines' failure to advance:

They [the Germans] are too strong for us. Soon as we take one machine gun, another opens. The losses are so heavy that I am reforming on the ground held by the 82d Company last night. All of the officers of the 82d Company wounded or missing and it is necessary to reform before we can advance. . . . We can attack again if desired.

Harbord decided against another attack that day. The battle then idled in deadlock. But the unseasoned marines had earned special attention from their veteran opponents.

Battle for Supremacy

Later that day, Major General von Haxthausen of the 5th Prussian Guards issued a report to his division stating:

A Surgeon Reports

Marine casualties in Belleau Wood piled up at an alarming rate, challenging the best efforts of stretcher bearers, medical corpsmen, ambulance drivers, and surgeons to accommodate and administer to the wounded. In his log entry for June 6, 1918, one unidentified battle surgeon noted:

Advance dressing stations established just behind first line where wounded were collected and ambulatory [walking wounded] sent to the battalion [aid] station. Litter cases transported a distance of about 500 yards. At the battalion station examinations and sorting done. [Those] evacuated from battalion go through regimental aid station where a check on each case is made. Returning ambulances bring fresh supplies, litters and blankets, so at no time have we been short of these necessities. Some cases of diarrhea developing. Only a few evacuations because of sickness made. The Second Battalion station located in Lucy le Bocage. Their position enabled them to care for all casualties of their battalion in line. Lucy likewise was under heavy shellfire and gas. A direct hit on this station set the building on fire, necessitating evacuation. A new station soon established in a cellar, and evacuations continued from this point. . . .

The character of wounds encountered here fall chiefly into tearing, lacerating [deep, irregular cutting], crushing, and amputating types, accompanied by all degrees of fractures, hemorrhage [heavy or uncontrollable bleeding], and destruction of soft tissue. Injuries of the extremities were most common, followed by those of the abdomen and chest. Despite massive injury, shock has not been common. This is probably due to early treatment, given by company hospital corpsmen, and undelayed evacuation through the regiment to field hospitals. Great attempts have been made to control hemorrhage, immobilize fractures, secure adequate dressings on all wounds, give morphine [painkiller], antitetanic [antitetanus] serum, hot coffee, cover patients with blankets, and promptly evacuate them from the area.

Despite the gallant efforts of all available medical personnel, their numbers were not sufficient to cope with the stream of wounded that crowded the dressing stations and field hospitals after the first attack on Belleau Wood. Surgeons worked in blood and primitive conditions around the clock to save as many of the maimed as possible. Even so, some of the wounded died before doctors could attend to them.

One of an alarming number of wounded is carried away in an ambulance. Medical personnel were in short supply, especially after the first phase of the battle.

The enemy intends to gain the following things: immobilization of the German forces and local improvement of his line. It will also give the Americans an opportunity for cheap successes. These are then to be headlined in the newspapers. It will be said that *one* American division [the 2d Division] has been sufficient to stop the German attacks without difficulty. . . . Should the Americans on our front gain the upper hand even temporarily, this may have the most unfavorable influence on the morale of the Central Powers and on the continuation of the war. In the fighting that faces us, therefore, it is not a matter of possession or non-possession of a village or a wood, of indifferent value in itself, but a question of whether English-American publicity will succeed in presenting the American army as one equal to the German army or as actually superior troops. The renewed employment of the 5th Guard and the 28th Infantry divisions in the front line of Corps Conta is to be considered from this point of view.

At this point, the battle at Belleau Wood took on a new dimension, discounting the limited value of the terrain in question and emphasizing the psychological aspects of winning and losing—and neither side wanted to lose. It became a battle for supremacy of forces, and its outcome would change the course of the world.

Slight Losses

On the night of June 8, Major John A. "Johnny the Hard" Hughes, now commanding the 1st Battalion, 6th Marines, moved his marines in south of Belleau Wood and relieved Sibley's exhausted troops. Sibley came off-line with losses of four hundred men, counting dead, wounded, and missing. Timmerman's platoon came away with nineteen survivors. Not one officer in 82d Company remained fit for action. At the same time, Major Shearer, taking over for the wounded Berry, moved up with the 3d Battalion, 5th Marines, and relieved Holcomb's 2d Battalion, 6th Marines, to the right of Hughes and in Bouresches.

On June 9, the French and Americans bombarded Belleau Wood with a thunderous artillery barrage throughout the day, turning once great trees into kindling. Desolation and death pervaded the atmosphere within the former hunting preserve. The German artillery blasted back with its own brand of destruction, shelling Lucy and Bouresches and everywhere in between. Inside Belleau Wood, the German infantry reorganized its defenses and braced for the next American attack. It came at 4:30 A.M. on June 10.

General Harbord ordered Hughes's 1st Battalion and some of Major Edward B. Cole's 6th Machine Gun Battalion into action. The attack moved smoothly at first. But German machine-gun fire stopped Hughes's marines and the 75th Machine Gun Company by 7:00 A.M. Major Cole was mortally wounded. Hughes, confused and misinformed in the midst of the heavy fighting, sent a report to brigade headquarters that all his objectives had been achieved.

(Above) A marine signal station attempts to communicate troop movements to commanders in the field. Difficulty in communication was one reason that Colonel Wise (bottom) thought he had orders to attack from the south, rather than the west.

General Harbord, also a victim of the continuing confusion and misinformation that often rules the battlefield, had seriously underestimated German strength inside the wood. At 2:44 P.M., Harbord telephoned a brief report to division headquarters:

> The attack started at 4:30 A.M. after a thorough artillery preparation. The objective was reached by 5:10 A.M. and since that hour is being consolidated. So far as known no prisoners were taken, but two large minenwerfers [trench mortars] were captured. Our losses were slight.

The marine losses numbered eight killed and twenty-four wounded. Harbord then decided to continue the attack. At 5:45 P.M., he issued Field Order Number Four.

Moving into Mayhem

The order called for Wise's 2d Battalion, 5th Marines, to attack the middle of the wood from the west, while Hughes's 1st Battalion, 6th Marines, was assaulting from the south. H-Hour was set for 4:30 A.M. the next day.

Wise had already lost 25 percent of his men. He and his marines were tired from days and nights of fighting and shelling. Wise, rightly or wrongly, thought Harbord had ordered him to attack the wood from the *south*. (This was a disputed order. Wise always insisted that Harbord had directed his battalion to attack from the south—definitely *not* from the west.)

Early in the evening of June 10, Wise briefed his company commanders on the forthcoming attack. Lieutenant Bill Mathews, Wise's intelligence officer, was present:

Paris in the Springtime

In early June 1918, only a thin line of marines at Belleau Wood blocked the advance of the mighty German army on Paris, the French capital and City of Light. A mere forty miles separated Parisians from the horrors of the front lines. But those in Paris that spring did not totally escape the long reach of Germany's military arm. In a personal letter written on June 8, Lee Meriweather, an official at the American embassy, told of Paris in the springtime of 1918:

> During the last week Paris has lived through seven frightfully anxious days—the 75-mile guns dropping shells on the city daily and Gothas [large aircraft] dropping bombs almost nightly. . . . A giant Gotha was captured a few nights ago; thinking they were inside their lines the Germans came to earth just in the rear of Betz where fortunately French soldiers were close enough at hand to capture the eight aviators and their machine, the wings of which have an expanse of 136 feet! The monster carried several tons of bombs, one of which weighed 2200 pounds! . . . Terrific fighting is still going on barely 40 miles from here where I am writing these notes; thus far the enemy is being "held," but whether he will continue to be held, or whether he will succeed in advancing again, and near enough to put Paris within reach of his marine guns [long-range naval cannon], remains to be seen. Yesterday the French government appointed a "Committee for the Defense of Paris." It announced that this is only a precaution and that the public must not become alarmed or imagine that the government believes the Germans will really enter the capital, or that they will even come close enough to bomb it with ordinary big cannon.

How close the Germans would come to the French capital depended upon the fighting qualities of the U.S. 2d Division—more specifically, the 4th Marine Brigade. As for the Germans, they had every intention of enjoying the fabled splendors of Paris in the springtime.

Captured German guns lie in the streets of Paris, France. Many historians credit the marines for the fact that the Germans did not take Paris.

The battalion was to attack at 4:30 A.M. through the big open space at the south end of the woods with the 43d Company [Captain Dunbeck's] on the left in two waves and the 51st Company [Captain Williams's] on the right in two waves. . . . The 51st was to attack due north and when it hit the road in the woods to follow it to the edge of the woods, detach one platoon to clear out the woods (a small clump) that was alongside of the Belleau-Bouresches road, while the rest of the company was to turn west and bear down on Hill 133 with the hope of taking the Germans from the rear and making a bag of prisoners. The 43d was to attack due north, but it had more woods to clear out . . . they were not expected to make as rapid progress as the 51st.

On June 11, Wise's 43d and 51st Companies moved out in darkness. Passing through freshly plowed wheat fields and shrouded by a thick morning mist, they approached Belleau Wood from the *south*. The lead companies quickly drew heavy rifle fire. Marines started dropping all along their line of skirmishers. Lieutenant Sam Cummings, a platoon leader with 51st Company, described the mayhem in a letter afterward:

> Line after line moved toward the woods six hundred yards away across an open and level field. The ground became covered by a sheet of machine gun fire. . . . Men were being mowed down like wheat. A whiz-bang [high-explosive shell] hit on my right and an automatic rifle team disappeared, while men on left and right were armless, legless, or tearing at their faces.

Captain Lloyd Williams, of 51st Company, took an early hit and died that night. The marines pressed on.

Going on Guts

Once inside the wood, the marines again faced the terror of interlocking bands of machine-gun fire. Scattered platoons and smaller units struggled through the dense underbrush and raking fire to weed out the enemy and close with him.

The fiercest fighting erupted along the eastern edge of the wood, where the marines slammed into the 40th Fusilier Regiment of the German 28th Infantry Division. The fusiliers lost more than seven hundred killed and wounded. Their regimental battle report later depicted the marines as having attacked in "gangs of ten to twenty men, primed with alcohol." The report continued:

> Some of their wounded kept on in the attack. . . . They had no idea of tactical principles. They fired while walking with their rifles under their arms. They carried light machine guns with them—no hand grenades, but knives, revolvers, rifle butts and bayonets. All were big fellows, powerful, rowdies. . . . It will hardly be possible to hold Belleau Wood in the event of a renewed hostile attack.

In the confusion of battle—often called the "fog of war"—Wise's troops could not find Hughes's and were forced to abandon plans to link up and sweep the woods. The terrain and the situation simply defied definition in marine experience, as Wise would later write:

> Nothing in all our training had foreseen fighting like this. If there was any strategy in it, it was the strategy of the Red Indian. The only thing that drove the Marines through those woods in the face of such resistance as they met was their individual, elemental guts, plus the hardening of the training through which they had gone.

Without landmarks to guide them through the wood, Wise's marines became disoriented and moved straight across the wood's narrow midsection rather than bearing northeast as had been intended. In the mix-up, Wise's left-hand companies—Captain Charles Dunbeck's 43d and Captain Lester Wass's 18th—ended up where his right-hand companies should have been. When the fighting dwindled, Wise, as had Hughes before him, reported all objectives achieved.

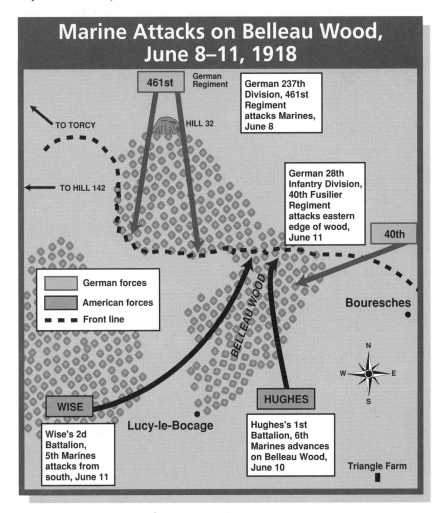

Marine Attacks on Belleau Wood, June 8–11, 1918

461st — German Regiment

German 237th Division, 461st Regiment attacks Marines, June 8

TO TORCY

HILL 32

German 28th Infantry Division, 40th Fusilier Regiment attacks eastern edge of wood, June 11

40th

TO HILL 142

German forces
American forces
Front line

BELLEAU WOOD

Bouresches

N W E S

WISE

HUGHES

Lucy-le-Bocage

Wise's 2d Battalion, 5th Marines attacks from south, June 11

Hughes's 1st Battalion, 6th Marines advances on Belleau Wood, June 10

Triangle Farm

The barrages of huge artillery shells that fell on Belleau Wood created a barren, crater-pocked landscape.

The Dogs of War

At 7:00 A.M., General Harbord, as a result of misconceptions and miscommunications, issued a false report: "The northern end of the *Bois de Belleau* belongs to the 5th Marines." A big mistake. Wise's 2d Battalion was still struggling in the south and had yet to enter the northern section of the wood. Wise did not learn the true situation until early that afternoon when he personally inspected his battalion's positions.

But Wise's marines were definitely making their presence felt in the wood's southern section, as indicated in a letter written by German private Hebel on June 11:

> We are having very heavy days with death before us hourly. Here we have no hope ever to come out. My company has been reduced from 120 to 30 men. . . . We are now at the worst stage of the offensive, the time of counter-attacks. We have Americans (Marines) opposite us who are very reckless fellows. In the last eight days I have not slept 20 hours.

One German dispatch from the front referred to the marines as *Teufelhünden*—Devil Dogs. To the everlasting pride of the U.S. Marine Corps, the name stuck.

CHAPTER SEVEN

Mustard Gas and Raw Guts

After dark on June 11, the Germans set up a new defense line in the wood—in front of Wise and on his right flank—and started pouring in reinforcements. Wise had by then lost half of his 2d Battalion, 5th Marines. Engineers and marine replacements moved on-line during the night. Since by this time General Pershing's headquarters had announced the capture of Belleau Wood to the world, it now fell to the marines to make good on the news. Much fighting remained to be done. Early on the morning of June 12, Wise again inspected his battalion:

> The woods had been cleared of all the wounded. The dead still lay where they fell. I was much better satisfied with the line: Those engineers and replacements had helped. It was well sprinkled with machine guns now—our own and captured German weapons. I wasn't afraid, then, of any breakthrough.

Later that morning, Wise met with General Harbord, Colonel Neville, and Lieutenant Colonel Logan Feland, Neville's second in command (of the 5th Marines), and reported his findings. A 2d Division record of the meeting indicated that Wise

> expressed the opinion that with a certain amount of artillery preparation he could capture the remainder of the Bois de Belleau. Accordingly it was arranged that artillery play on the north-western section of the Bois de Belleau until 5 P.M. when an attack is to be made. In this connection verbal orders were given to the 12th Field Artillery.

A ruined village outside Belleau Wood highlights the fact that World War I fighting did not take place on orderly battlefields but was carved out of areas that had once been bucolic country villages.

Surprisingly, Harbord still believed that German resistance was light and allowed Wise to prepare for an attack that afternoon—even though Wise's battalion was dead tired, battered, and still understrength. Apparently both Harbord and Wise felt compelled to make amends for prematurely reporting that Belleau Wood had been cleared of Germans.

Bullets and Bayonets

This time the assault was to be led by army Lieutenant E. D. Cooke's 55th Company, Dunbeck's 43d, and Wass's 18th. Cooke, an army officer on loan to Wise's battalion, had assumed command of 55th Company upon the death of Captain John Blanchfield. Again, Hughes's 1st Battalion was to attack from the south, as Wise's 2d Battalion was striking from the west.

The start of the attack was delayed until 5:30 P.M. for additional artillery preparation. Because of misinformation as to the marines' location, the pre-attack barrage struck a thousand yards too far in advance of them and failed to take out the Germans closest to the marines. The unharmed Germans met the marine attack with all of their available weaponry. "The Boche heard us coming and gave us all they had," wrote Lieutenant Cooke, adding some lucid details:

> Light machine guns camouflaged in trees, heavy guns on the ground, grenades, rifles, pistols; everything was turned loose at once. In front of me Sergeant Brown was bent nearly double, pulling his men forward with beckoning arms. A burst of

bullets burst into a man's jaw beside me, carrying away the lower part of his face. A grenade fell on the other side, tearing a youngster's legs to shreds.

Still, the marines charged forward, shouting and screaming like souls possessed, and entered the gates of the damned. Hand-to-hand, no-quarter-asked-or-given combat with rifle, pistol, and bayonet followed. During the action, Private Aloysius Leitner, of Captain Lester Wass's 18th Company, despite mortal wounds, fought off death long enough to help capture six Germans operating a machine gun. Lieutenant Colonel Wise later documented the actions of Leitner and other members of his squad:

> One squad of his company, Wass told me, had taken a German machine gun camouflaged behind a brush pile in the middle of the woods, that day. The minute they got among the Germans with bayonets, the Germans, who had worked the gun up to that minute and had cut up the Marines pretty badly, surrendered. The Marines took them all prisoners. Not one was killed. And that minute another German machine gun opened up on their flank. They left their prisoners, charged the second gun, and captured it. The minute they got among those Germans with bayonets, every one of them surrendered. And that minute the captured gun crew they had left behind them opened fire on them again. They couldn't play back and forth like this all day. They bayoneted every man of that second German gun crew, went back and captured the first gun all over again, and bayoneted every man of that crew before they went on.

Captured German soldiers stare defiantly at the camera. In spite of the fierce fighting at Belleau Wood, prisoners were taken in a humane fashion.

"Wild-Eyed and Panting"

The marines attacked the stubborn Germans again and again in Belleau Wood. The marines' fight to wrench possession of the former hunting preserve from the Germans turned into a hand-to-hand struggle. Lieutenant E. D. Cooke, company commander of 55th Company, wrote later of the June 12 fighting and actions typical of the marines' kill-or-be-killed way of fighting:

> We crushed the Germans' forward line and reached the ravine and clearing where [Lieutenant Edgar] Poe and I had stood the previous day. . . . The hostile fire we had undergone up 'til then was only a preliminary to what we received from across the clearing. One of my lieutenants went down, writhing and clawing at his face, begging to be gotten out of there. A sergeant ducked behind the tree next to mine just as a bullet hit and exploded the canteen on his belt. We both thought we were drenched with blood.

> Then, in the field to our left, from where they [the Germans] had been working around our flank, a group of gray-clad figures got up like a covey of frightened quail. Big, husky Huns, running over the [plowed] ground with stilted awkwardness in their heavy boots.

> For a stupefied moment I stared with open mouth, then, clawing out my automatic, I let go an entire clip at their retreating backs. The whole company discharged a scattered volley—and we never hit a damn one!

> From over to the right came a stirring yell. Sergeant Colvin of the 18th Company was going up the side of a rocky cliff after a machine gun, like a cat chasing birds on a tin roof. Still nearer was [Captain] Wass, pursuing a frightened Heinie over a pile of cordwood.

> "Eyah!" one of the 43d Company men suddenly screamed . . . the kids were startled by that yell. Fear, hunger, fatigue—everything seemed forgotten in a mad lust to ram two feet of steel into some Heinie's innards.

> Out in the open they surged, and much against my better judgment I was carried along in the excitement. Down into the ravine—our momentum carrying us half way up the opposite side.

> The hot blast of guns beat against our faces, grenades curved over our heads, underbrush and men dying clogged our feet. We pounded across a road, crashed into some thickets bordering the clearing and stood, wild-eyed and panting.

> The Boche had slipped into the underbrush and run.

Leitner was posthumously awarded both the Distinguished Service Cross and the Navy Cross for his contributions.

Celebration

The marines then began to shove the Germans back, northward through the rocks and crevices of Belleau Wood. On their right, the marines succeeded in pushing them clear out of the wood. But other German elements kept fighting. Suddenly, the entire marine line erupted in a hail of exploding shells bearing high explosives and mustard gas. Captain Edward C. Fuller, the company commander of 75th Company (and the son of future marine commandant Benjamin H. Fuller), was mortally wounded.

At 3:00 A.M., June 13, the Germans lashed out at the wood's eastern side and at Bouresches, where Shearer's 3d Battalion, 5th Marines, stopped them cold in a grim turkey shoot. Early that same morning, Turrill's 1st Battalion had moved into the wood to search out Wise and bear a hand in the western sector. But Wise was still in the southern end of the wood and not where he was thought to be. Instead of Wise, Shearer found the wood's west side unexpectedly full of Germans.

Late that afternoon, General Harbord ordered Major Holcomb's 2d Battalion, 6th Marines, into the wood to relieve Wise's decimated 2d Battalion, 5th Marines. Before Holcomb could comply, the Germans unleashed a crippling mustard-gas attack on his marines. Holcomb had just entered the wood on an advance inspection tour of Wise's position when the bombardment broke. Wise later described what happened next:

> We started out from my P.C. on the same route I took on my regular morning inspection. It was about 5 P.M. We had hardly left my P.C. when the Germans cut loose with a bombardment that, while it wasn't quite as heavy as the one we had stood the night before, still was heavy enough. Hundred-and-fifty-fives [155mm] and seventy-sevens [77mm] began to burst up and down the line. On top of them, the whizbangs [German 77mm] came smashing through. Splintered trees were torn into still smaller splinters. Great masses of earth

U.S. Marines in France perform a gas mask drill.

Major Holcomb's troops arrived in Belleau Wood in the middle of such vicious German fire that he quipped, "Is this celebration due to my arrival?"

and roots, of limbs and fragments of trunks, mixed with shell-fragments themselves, began to fly through the air. The din was deafening—a solid, continuous roar.

Holcomb looked at me. "Is this celebration due to my arrival?" he shouted in my ear.

"No," I shouted back. "This is only routine."

We flopped right where we stood when the shelling started and lay flat against the ground until it ended a half hour later. Then we went on with the inspection.

Holcomb returned to his battalion, bivouacked in a wheat field southeast of Lucy, and alerted his men that they would move into the wood in relief of Wise's battalion at midnight.

Close Call

Shortly before midnight, Lieutenant Clifton B. Cates, now company commander of Holcomb's 96th Company, donned his awkward combat equipment and started assembling his men to move out:

> I had not gone twenty feet from my fox hole when I heard a salvo of shells heading our way. From the whistle I thought they were gas shells, and when they hit with a thud and no detonation [explosion] my fears were confirmed. Soon I smelled the gas, and I gave the alarm to the men, and they all put on their masks. By this time there was already a steady stream of incoming shells—gas, air bursts [shells with fuses timed to explode above ground], shrapnel, and high explosives. I reached for my gas mask, but it wasn't there. Naturally, I was petrified. I tried to find my hole where I had left it, but I became confused and couldn't locate it.

A less experienced person might have panicked in a similar situation, but Cates forced himself to remain cool. He recalled that one of his men, Private Hall, had picked up a German gas mask as a souvenir. With the caustic fumes of mustard gas fast growing intolerable around him, Cates called to Hall. Hall answered, "Here I am, over here. What do you—"

Cates jumped into Hall's foxhole before the private could finish his sentence and put on the captured mask. The mask, although too small, was large enough to cover Cates's mouth, nose, and eyes, which was sufficient to spare him an agonizing, choking death. The future commandant survived a very close call.

Hellhole

The German artillery continued to pound away at the marines. "The shelling was so heavy we didn't try to move out," Cates recalled, "which I now realize was a mistake." Cates explained:

"Someone Laughed!"

No human being can withstand for long the horrors of close combat and the landscapes of desolation and death without courting madness. Mercifully, after two weeks of fierce fighting, the 7th Infantry Regiment of the U.S. 3d Division relieved the 4th Marine Brigade for a much needed rest. Lieutenant E. D. Cooke later described the torment of battle and the elation of survival:

> My nerves were completely shot. I cowered in a foxhole at the sound of every shell and cringed at any unexpected noise. If a man had suddenly yelled in my ear I'd have probably shot him dead. [Lieutenant] Jackson came through on the way to the hospital and I thought him lucky.

> Then, on the night of June 15th, our whole outfit was relieved. Another battalion was to finish what we were too few to accomplish. My company, with some of the 43d [Company] attached, filed silently back through the spectral forest and the ruins that had once been Lucy. Stealthily we slipped past buildings that were tumbled to the ground, under beams reared on end, around shell holes gaping in the streets. Smoke eddied about our feet while gas clung to the broken walls and dripped from crevices.

> We kept no formation. Each man simply followed the one in front. No one was going to let himself be left behind. We wanted to hurry but our legs acted as gripped by an undertow. Weak, starved, and apprehensive we bent forward, painfully propelling ourselves up the hill from Lucy, pathetically eager for escape.

> But shells suddenly dropped along the road. The battle reached out, diabolically determined not to let us go. . . . We plodded on, praying for no more shells. Just a little longer and we would be beyond their reach. With each step, we gained confidence and strength. Someone laughed! We hadn't heard a laugh for days. Someone whistled! Well, why not? We were safe. Safe! They hadn't gotten us that time. No, by God, we'd fooled 'em.

> It kept up for hours, and we suffered rather heavy casualties, both from shell fragments and gas, as many of our masks were defective. Heroes were made that night, as the wounded had to be carried to the dressing [medical] station, which was under a stone bridge down the ravine. Many of the stretcher bearers were hit while carrying the wounded. As soon as the Boche artillery fire stopped, we moved out with about half of the company remaining, and went into this hell hole Belleau Woods.

All told, the Germans dumped seven thousand mustard-gas bombs and more than two thousand high-explosive shells containing a vomiting and sneezing agent on Holcomb's marines. His battalion took 160 casualties from the gas.

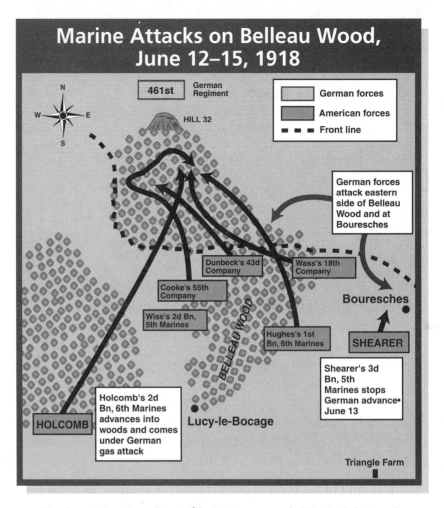

Marine Attacks on Belleau Wood, June 12–15, 1918

461st German Regiment

HILL 32

German forces
American forces
Front line

German forces attack eastern side of Belleau Wood and at Bouresches

Dunbeck's 43d Company

Wass's 18th Company

Cooke's 55th Company

Wise's 2d Bn, 5th Marines

BELLEAU WOOD

Hughes's 1st Bn, 6th Marines

Bouresches

SHEARER

Shearer's 3d Bn, 5th Marines stops German advance June 13

Holcomb's 2d Bn, 6th Marines advances into woods and comes under German gas attack

HOLCOMB

Lucy-le-Bocage

Triangle Farm

Hughes's 1st Battalion, 6th Marines, and Wise's 2d Battalion, 5th Marines, also fell under heavy gas attack. The breath-stifling, lung-searing gas forced the evacuation of the 74th, 78th, and 96th Companies of the 6th Marines.

During the gassing, Gunnery Sergeant Fred W. Stockham, of 96th Company, gave up his gas mask to save a wounded marine whose mask had been shot away. Stockham paid the ultimate price for his act of raw courage, dying a few days after inhaling the lethal mustard fumes. He received the Medal of Honor posthumously.

An Unsurpassed Record

The action subsided temporarily on June 14. Allied leaders reviewed battle strategy, and General Harbord reorganized his brigade. At the same time, General Degoutte took command of the French 6th Army Corps, replacing General Duchêne.

Finally, on the morning of June 15, Captain Roswell Winans's 17th Company, of Turrill's 1st Battalion, 5th Marines, established a firm foothold on the western side of the wood. Late in the day and into the night, the 7th Infantry Regiment, of the U.S. 3d Division, came on-line to relieve the embattled marines. The bearded and bedraggled troops of the 4th Marine Brigade, after serving stern notice of American fighting capabilities to the Germans, moved to the rear for a hard-earned rest.

Lieutenant Colonel Fritz Wise and Captain Lester Wass, his sole remaining officer (who was killed two months later), inspected the 2d Battalion, 5th Marines, on the morning of June 16. Of the ragtag survivors of his battalion, Wise later wrote:

> It was enough to break your heart. I had left . . . on May 31 with 965 men and 26 officers. Now, before me, stood 350 men and 6 officers. . . . For 17 days they hadn't had a cup of hot coffee or a bite of hot food. They hadn't taken off their shoes. They hadn't had a chance to wash their faces. . . . But they had driven trained German veterans out of fortified positions by frontal attack; had walked into the fiercest kind of woods fighting in France; had taken nearly twice their own number in German prisoners and captured more than 50 machine-guns. . . . They had made a record unsurpassed in war.

Despite the tenacious efforts of the marines so far, however, sole possession of Belleau Wood remained in dispute.

Seal of Approval

General Harbord's brigade of marines had taken a severe pounding and there was more punishment to come. If the general felt depressed over his losses, Colonel Neville helped to lift his spirits during one of Harbord's morning visits. Neville handed his commander a pair of Marine Corps eagle-globe-and-anchor collar emblems and said, "Here, we think it is about time you put these on." This simple act by a marine in his command touched Harbord deeply. He later said:

> I was as much thrilled by his brusque remark and his subsequent pinning them on my collar the next few minutes as I have ever been by any decoration of the several that have come to me. I wore those Marine Corps devices until after I became a Major General, and I still cherish them as among my most valued possessions. I think no officer can fail to understand what that little recognition meant to me, an Army officer commanding troops of a sister service in battle. It seemed to me to set the seal of approval by my comrades of the Marine Corps, and knowing the circumstances, it meant everything to me.

When a person joins the Marine Corps, he or she is not considered a *marine* until completing recruit training, thereby earning the right to wear the Marine Corps emblem. To wear the emblem

Although usually a fierce rivalry exists between divisions of the military—especially the U.S. Army and the marines—General Harbord was accepted by the marines he fought alongside. In appreciation, the marines gave him a set of Marine Corps eagle-globe-and-anchor collar emblems.

Surviving officers of the 2d Battalion, 6th Marines, take a brief rest from their duties during the Battle of Belleau Wood. Included in this photo, from left to right, are Erskine (fourth from left), and Holcomb (seventh from left).

means that one has passed the qualifying test for becoming a marine. Neville and the marines could have paid no finer tribute to their commanding officer.

Unshaken Spirit

During two weeks of intensive action, the 4th Marine Brigade had suffered more than 50 percent casualties—enough to shake the spirit of any fighting organization. Yet, General Harbord trusted in his faithful marines and remained outwardly optimistic. He informed General Bundy:

> I am very glad to report that not withstanding their physical exhaustion, which is almost total, and the adverse circumstances of gas, the spirit of the Brigade remains unshaken.

In the ranks of the 5th Marines, Turrill's 1st Battalion had lost 16 officers and 544 men; Wise's 2d Battalion, 20 officers and 615 men. As for the 6th Marines, Holcomb's 2d Battalion had absorbed losses of 21 officers and 836 men; Sibley's 3d Battalion, 14 officers and 400 men.

While the marines recuperated in the rear, adding more than twenty-eight hundred replacements to their ranks, the Germans moved a new battalion into Belleau Wood. The enemy now held the northern section of the wood with renewed strength and vigor.

The "unshaken" spirit of the 4th Marine Brigade would be needed in the days ahead.

CHAPTER EIGHT

"Belleau Woods Now U.S. Marine Corps Entirely"

During the six days from June 16 through June 22, the Germans held the untested troops of the 7th Infantry Regiment to a standstill. On June 18, General Harbord received word that the soldiers were digging in deeper and improving their barbed-wire defenses. Harbord sent a curt message to Lieutenant Colonel Adams, commander of the regiment's 1st Battalion:

> It is understood that you are wiring an east and west line through the woods between you and the party of Germans on whom you are supposed to exert pressure. It is not believed that you have anything to fear from any aggression on the part of these people and it is not desired that you wire yourself in to prevent the pressure which it is desired you exert steadily until these people are killed or driven out.

Adams's Company D mounted a small attack with two platoons on June 20 that resulted in sixty-three American casualties and failed to gain any ground. Harbord informed 2d Division headquarters:

> Attack ordered on machine gun nest of northwestern edge of Bois de Belleau failed because companies of 7th Infantry fell back when a few [actually many] casualties occurred. One company commander . . . relieved by Battalion Commander for inefficiency and sent to report to Regimental Commander.

Harbord had apparently chosen to ignore growing signs that the enemy was stronger than intelligence reports had indicated. And he further failed to concede that the newly arrived, inexperienced 7th Infantry Regiment might lack the drive and resolve needed for an

(Above) Marines rest before moving to the front lines of Belleau Wood. (Below) Major Shearer was ordered to clean the Germans out of Belleau Wood. The orders were wildly optimistic.

all-out, final assault. Harbord ordered another attack for the morning of June 21. His harsh order to Lieutenant Colonel Adams stated:

> Your battalion will be relieved tomorrow night. Tomorrow morning is its only chance to redeem the failure made this morning. If you clear the northern half of Bois de Belleau the credit will belong to the 1st Battalion, 7th Infantry, and will be freely given. The battalion cannot afford to fail again.

The attack commenced at 3:15 the next morning. At 7:30 A.M., the 1st Battalion soldiers withdrew to their original positions. The attack had failed almost before it had begun.

The Last Failure

General Harbord ordered Major Shearer's 3d Battalion, 5th Marines, back into Belleau Wood to clean out the Germans once and for all. Harbord continued to underestimate German strength.

On June 23, Shearer jumped off at 7:00 P.M. without benefit of artillery to prepare the way. A heavy concentration of German machine guns chopped up the marines badly. Shearer quickly took 130 casualties. Lieutenant Laurence Stallings, a platoon leader with the supporting 47th Company, later described the grim effects of advancing into hostile machine-gun fire:

Undelivered Mail

The Americans experienced untold hardships and unspeakable terrors during the fighting for Belleau Wood, but the gods of war recognized no favorites. War's miseries applied equally to the common foot soldier on both sides of the lines. An unmailed letter taken from the body of a dead German infantryman in the Bois de Belleau attests to the equality of suffering on the firing line. Dated June 21, 1918, it reads:

> We are now in the battle zone and canteens [mobile field kitchens] dare not come to us on account of the enemy, for the Americans are bombarding the villages fifteen kilometers behind the present front with long-range guns, and you will know that the canteen outfit and the others who are lying in reserve do not venture very far, for it is not "pleasant to eat cherries" ["socialize," that is, do battle] with the Americans. The reason for that is that they have not yet had much experience. The American divisions are still too fiery. They are the first divisions that the French have entered. . . . We will also show the Americans how good we are, for the day before yesterday we bombarded them heavily with our gas. About 400 of us are lying around here. We have one corner of the woods and the American has the other. That is not nice, for all of a sudden he rushes forward and one does not know it beforehand. Therefore, one must shoot at every little noise, for one cannot trust them. Here always two men have dug a hold [emplacement] for themselves. Here one lies day and night without a blanket, only with a coat and a shelter-half. One freezes at night like a tailor, for the nights are fiercely cold. I hope that I will be lucky enough to escape from this horrible mess, for up to now I have always been lucky. Many of my comrades are already buried here. The enemy sweeps every evening the whole countryside with machine gun and rifle fire, and then artillery fire. But we in [the] front line are safer than in the support position. At present our food is miserable. We are now fed upon dried vegetables and marmalade and when at night we obtain more food it is unpalatable. It is half sour and all cold. In the daytime we receive nothing.

Men in supporting platoons, inching forward to plug the gaps in a decimated company where there was no artillery roar to drown the cries of human beings, sometimes thought this duty the worst of war's alarms. The cries of men as blood drained from them and they lost self-control were almost not to be endured. Officers restraining men who wished to administer first aid to such sufferers felt themselves unconscionable brutes as they hazed the kindhearted into gaps littered with corpses, crawling forward hugging the ground, the blood of other men on their sleeves, their hands, their faces. Wounded lads on their backs, a kneecap still on its ligaments caught in brambles where it had been shot out of a leg, begging for someone to release it so they might inch back farther to some slight depression, might find succor; but the ones who needed tourniquets and compresses—and precious time—could not be accommodated. The gaps had to be plugged. This last failure in Belleau Wood would be remembered by some as the worst afternoon of their lives no matter what fortune later befell them.

The 3d Battalion ground to a bloody halt in the sad consequence of an ill-conceived operation.

Going Through

The entire marine brigade returned to the front on June 24. The 5th Marines deployed Shearer's 3d Battalion in the middle of the wood, with the 2d Battalion, under Lieutenant Colonel Ralph S. Keyser (who had replaced Lieutenant Colonel Wise), on Shearer's left. (Harbord had severely criticized Wise's performance. Wise subsequently exploded, and Harbord relieved him.) The 6th Marines installed Sibley's 3d Battalion on Shearer's right, thus extending the line to Bouresches. The three remaining battalions (Holcomb, Turrill, and Hughes) were held in reserve.

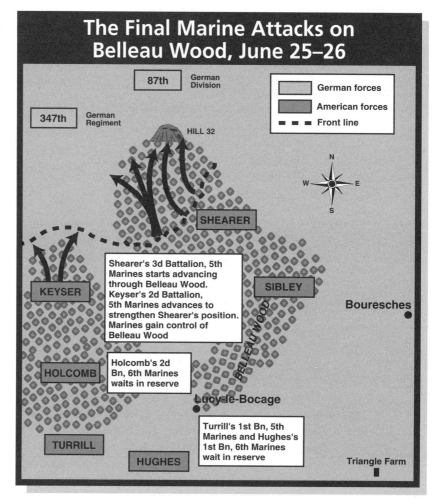

The Final Marine Attacks on Belleau Wood, June 25–26

87th — German Division

347th — German Regiment

HILL 32

German forces
American forces
Front line

N W E S

SHEARER

KEYSER

SIBLEY

Bouresches

BELLEAU WOOD

Shearer's 3d Battalion, 5th Marines starts advancing through Belleau Wood. Keyser's 2d Battalion, 5th Marines advances to strengthen Shearer's position. Marines gain control of Belleau Wood

Holcomb's 2d Bn, 6th Marines waits in reserve

HOLCOMB

Lucy-le-Bocage

Turrill's 1st Bn, 5th Marines and Hughes's 1st Bn, 6th Marines wait in reserve

TURRILL

HUGHES

Triangle Farm

The Heroes of June

In his memoirs of *The American Army in France*, Brigadier General James G. Harbord recalled the gallant warriors who fought in Belleau Wood and the surrounding area in June 1918:

> The heroes of that month in front of the enemy sprang from every racial strain that has contributed to our national life. . . . The wounds from which they suffered and some died, and the sacrifices they made were as varied as the instrumentalities with which men make modern war. Remaining at the front when wounded, until carried back or compelled by orders to go, was a common case. Rushing out under withering fire to rescue a fallen comrade, carrying him sometimes hundreds of yards to safety was so frequent as to be the expected thing. Taking over command of a unit at the death or disabling wounds of all seniors and instantly rising to the responsibilities thus assumed was the rule of the hour. . . . Runners shot as they ran with messages and reports, and dragging themselves with broken legs or other disabling injuries to insure the delivery of the message—it happened many times. The taking of a machine gun or its nest at the cost of a man's life was an ordinary sacrifice. The deeds of heroism came from all ranks and from all units. A lieutenant fresh from college and a veteran Marine [Lieutenant William B. Moore and Sergeant Major John H. Quick] together drive a truck loaded with ammunition, in open daylight down the shell and machine gun swept road to Bouresches. Many a man gives his life sheltering or carrying a comrade. Medical officers and men of both Army and Navy dress wounds under fire as coolly as if in an isolation ward in a city hospital. Field hospitals partly blown away by a shell leave the surgeon uninterrupted at the operating table. Men with eyes blinded by gas stay in line and keep the touch. Men with an arm or hand shot off carry on until they drop from shock or loss of blood. A soldier puts his foot on a hand grenade which there is not time to throw away, losing his foot but saving his comrades of the group. Seizing hand grenades to throw away often happened. Such are some of the deeds that cheered the Allied world.

A sea of helmets can be seen in this photo taken from a New York skyscraper during a victory parade for the U.S. Marines returning from the battlefields of World War I.

In Memoriam

The German army officer Lieutenant Colonel Ernst Otto concluded his excellent account in *The Battles for the Possession of Belleau Woods, 1918* with a suggestion to honor the dead:

On the edge of the blood-drenched woods . . . we might well erect a monument draped with the French, German, and American colors, and bearing the inscription:

THESE ARE THE WOODS OF BELLEAU; IN JUNE,
1918, WRESTED FROM THE FRENCH, AFTER A BRAVE
DEFENSE, BY THE GERMANS, STORMING ON IN A
BOLD TWO-DAY OFFENSIVE; HEROICALLY
DEFENDED BY THEM FOR NINE DAYS; THEN TAKEN
BY STORM IN TWO DAYS, WITH INCOMPARABLE
BRAVERY, BY THE AMERICANS, WHO REMAINED
VICTORIOUSLY IN POSSESSION OF THE WOODS.
HONOR TO THE UNEXCELLED HEROES OF THE
THREE NATIONS WHO,
TRUE TO THEIR FATHERLAND,
HERE FOUGHT AND DIED.

Row upon row of crosses decorate the American cemetery in Belleau Wood near Château-Thierry in mute evidence of the gallant lives laid down there.

On June 25, following a deafening, all-day artillery barrage, Shearer's battalion started advancing through the wood at 5:00 P.M. Shearer informed Harbord:

> Attack started O.K. at 5 P.M. Heavy firing on us just before we jumped off. Several casualties. Very little machine gun fire. Telephone line out. Runner reports 7 prisoners and one captain also prisoner, carrying back wounded. The two left platoons 16th Company reported grenades and snipers working on them. No report from companies yet. Will go through if humanly possible.

The American cannons had silenced the enemy machine guns, but the marines still absorbed heavy casualties. Enemy losses were also heavy, however, and the Germans were running out of replacements. They then began a forced withdrawal to the Belleau-Torcy road to the north of the wood.

At 8:40 P.M., Shearer dispatched an urgent message to Harbord, which said in part:

> Our casualties will make help necessary. Please keep artillery and machine guns going to stop reinforcements of the enemy.

Then, at 9:30 P.M., Shearer notified Harbord:

> We have taken practically all of woods but do need help to clean it up and hold it. Do we get it?

U.S. Marines fill a photo shortly after taking Belleau Wood.

To strengthen Shearer's position, General Harbord ordered Lieutenant Colonel Keyser to move his 2d Battalion forward. Shortly after 11:00 P.M., Harbord praised Shearer's 3d Battalion to Colonel Neville, regimental commander of the 5th Marines:

> Your Shearer battalion has done splendid work. I have no fear of a counter-attack by the Germans tonight. You are in charge of the Bois de Belleau and can divert such part of Major Sibley's [3d] Battalion [6th Marines] as you think best. His front is practically wired in. . . . Artillery are trying to neutralize some of the enemy artillery.

At 7:00 A.M. the next morning, Captain Robert Yowell's 16th Company, of Shearer's 3d Battalion, 5th Marines, reached the northern edge of the wood. Major Shearer dispatched a message to General Harbord: "Belleau Woods now U.S. Marine Corps entirely."

Depleted but Proud

While killing 150 Germans, taking some 300 prisoners, and capturing 30 machine guns, the 3d Battalion paid dearly for its accomplishments with 250 casualties. Holcomb's 2d Battalion, 6th Marines, moved in to relieve Shearer's depleted but proud battalion that evening.

The Great War would continue for several months, but Belleau Wood belonged, then and forever, to the U.S. Marines.

AFTERWORD

Bois de la Brigade de Marine

After the marine victory in the battle for Belleau Wood, the French Parliament declared July 4 a national holiday to honor Americans fighting on French soil. The 2d Division paraded in Paris amid cries of *"Vive les Marines!"*

General Pershing told the marines: "You stood like a wall against the enemy advance on Paris." Marshal Ferdinand Foch, the supreme commander of Allied forces, called Belleau Wood the "cradle of Victory."

The 6th Marine Regiment turns into the Champs Elysees during an Independence Day parade in Paris.

"The Glory of American Arms"

General John J. "Black Jack" Pershing, commander of the American Expeditionary Force in France, awarded the Distinguished Service Cross for bravery to more than a hundred marines who fought in Belleau Wood. To honor the battlefield accomplishments of the 2d Division, Pershing issued the following order:

> It is with inexpressible pride and satisfaction that your commander recounts your glorious deeds on the field of battle. In the early days of June on a front of twenty kilometers, after night marches and with only the reserve rations which you carried, you stood like a wall against the enemy advance on Paris. For this timely action you have received the thanks of the French people whose homes you saved and the generous praise of your comrades in arms.
>
> Since the organization of our sector, in the face of strong opposition, you have advanced your lines two kilometers on a front of eight kilometers. You have engaged and defeated with great loss three [actually four] German divisions and have occupied important strong points—Belleau Wood, Bouresches, and Vaux. You have taken about 1,400 prisoners, many machine guns, and much other material. The complete success of the infantry was made possible by the splendid co-operation of the artillery, by the aid and assistance of the engineer and signal troops, by the diligent and watchful care of the medical and supply services, and by the unceasing work of the well-organized staff.
>
> Amid the dangers and trials of battle, every officer and man has done well his part. Let the stirring deeds, hardships, and sacrifices of the past month remain forever a bright spot in our history. Let the sacred memory of our fallen comrades spur us on to renewed effort and to the glory of American arms.

French marshal Ferdinand Foch, left, wanted American troops to replace wounded or dead Allied soldiers. American general John J. Pershing wanted Americans to fight together, under American officers. Pershing got his way—and the marines added new blood and fighting spirit to the cause.

An Enemy Evaluation

Even the enemy paid tribute to the American 2d Division, particularly its two marine regiments. On August 17, 1918, General Richard von Conta, commanding general of the German Corps Conta, issued the following report:

> The 2d American may be described as a very good division, and might even be considered as fit for use as shock troops. The numerous attacks by the two marine regiments in Belleau Woods were executed vigorously and without regard for the consequences. Our fire did not affect their morale sufficiently to interfere appreciably with their advance; their nerves had not yet been used up. . . .

> In spirit the troops are lively and full of a grim but good-natured confidence. Indicative is the expression of a prisoner: "We kill or get killed."

The Finest Tribute

But perhaps the finest tribute paid to the marines came from Major General Jean M. J. Degoutte, commander of the French 6th Army. On June 30, 1918, Degoutte issued the following proclamation:

> In view of the brilliant conduct of the 4th Brigade of the 2d U.S. Division, which in a spirited fight took Bouresches and the important strong point of Belleau Wood, stubbornly defended by a large enemy force, the General commanding the 6th French Army orders that henceforth, in all official papers, the Bois de Belleau shall be named "Bois de la Brigade de Marine."

The little patch of wood with such a big history remains so named until this day. *"Vive les Marines!"*

"The Honors at the End"

In the fight for Bouresches and Belleau Wood, the marines exacted a heavy toll of casualties from their enemy and paid an enormous price in return. Brigadier General James G. Harbord, commander of the 4th Marine Brigade, later wrote:

> The Marine Brigade used up four German Divisions during its month of fighting in the Belleau Wood and captured about a thousand prisoners. It lost of its own strength six hundred and seventy killed and three thousand, seven hundred and twenty-one wounded on the sunny slopes of Hill 142, in the tangled thickets of the Wood, and in the narrow streets of Bouresches. . . .

French general Jean Degoutte was so impressed and grateful to the marines of Belleau Wood that he renamed the ground the Woods of the Marine Brigade.

The 4th of July

On July 4, 1918, the French held a great parade and grand celebration in Paris to honor Americans fighting in France. In a letter to his mother, Lieutenant Clifton B. Cates, a future commandant of the Marine Corps, described that festive occasion:

The morning of the 4th, we got up early and cleaned up and tried to look half way decent, but we still looked like a bunch of bums. At eight we left camp and marched to where the parade formed. Mother, you cannot imagine the cheer that would go up as the French people would recognize the Marine flag—Vive la Marines—la Marines, etc. They literally covered us with roses—I would carry each bouquet a piece and then drop it—then another girl would load me down with more flowers. It was truly wonderful and it made us Marines feel very good as they gave us all of the credit. Even every little kid going to and from Paris would yell, "Vive la Marines." We have certainly made a name in France. . . . Most of all Paris witnessed the parade, and it was one grand night and adventure for us—one that I will never forget. The parade ended at noon—then three hundred men and four officers and myself went out to the largest ammunition factory in the world for lunch. We rode out and first went through the factory. It was a wonderful big factory and employed 10,000 girls—a very good class of girls. . . . They gave us Marines another fine welcome as we filed through. We then marched into an enormous dining room. At each table there was an American ribbon on one chair so a soldier would sit at each table. We were above in the club rooms where we could look down on that angry [jokingly] mob—

U.S. Marines proudly march in the 4th of July parade given in their honor by the grateful French.

over 10,000 and mostly girls. . . . At each table there was red wine and champagne. It was wonderful to look at that mob in one dining room. They had a fine band and the dinner was swell. We had the same and we ate with a lot of generals, colonels, etc. Also a lot of pretty girls. At a given signal they twisted the wire on the champagne bottles and hit them on the tables—imagine two thousand corks popping about forty feet into the air all at once. It sounded like a German barrage. Of course, champagne flew in every direction. After filling the glasses, toasts were made and responded to. After lunch they set the chairs up on the table and danced for two hours—the girls literally fought over the men. After that we went back to our barracks and discarded our arms and went up town on liberty. Until 6 A.M. the next morning.

The Marine Brigade had added another name to Tripoli, Mexico and China, and a score of others that are written on the tablets of Marine history and immortalized in the traditions of the Corps. . . .

Over four thousand dead and wounded was a dear price to pay for a bit of French territory—but it was somewhat compensated for by the fact that the little bit of lovely France was at the very spearpoint of the German push for Paris. . . .

More than the Bois de Belleau was at stake in those June days. More indeed than standing between the invader and fair Paris. It was a struggle for psychological mastery. The man from overseas [the American] was untried in the eyes of his Allied world; the man from over the Rhine [the German] had the prestige of victory on a hundred fields. Who now would prove the master in stubborn day-by-day, hand-to-hand struggle? Who would first recoil when next they met? It was a small stage, perhaps, but the audience was the world of 1918. The odds in experience, in terrain and in prestige were with the German; the honors at the end lay with the American.

Harbord considered the June action at Belleau Wood vital because it enabled the Allies to turn the war around during the fighting that followed at Soissons in July 1918. But the battle also had its critics.

Last Words

As military professionals are prone to do, many disagreed as to the importance of Belleau Wood. In a letter to General John J. Pershing, Major General Tasker H. Bliss, military adviser to President Woodrow Wilson, wrote that "the American troops in the vicinity of Château-Thierry stopped the German drive and very possibly saved Paris."

Contrarily, General Matthew B. Ridgway, who later achieved fame in World War II and Korea, wrote that Belleau Wood was "one of many prize examples of men's lives being thrown away against objectives which were not worth the cost . . . a monument, for all time, to the inflexibility of military thinking in that period."

No doubt some of the criticisms of the battle were rooted in professional jealousies. Because the marines had garnered enormous publicity and

A soldier's sketch depicts the village of Belleau. In the foreground are shell holes that were occupied by the Germans. To the right is a row of American graves.

The Guns Fell Silent

Private Elton E. Macklin served as a runner with 67th Company, 1st Battalion, 5th Marines, in every World War I campaign in which the marine brigade took part. In his memoirs, *Suddenly We Didn't Want To Die,* the highly decorated Macklin recalled the final day of the war when the guns at last fell silent:

> Rifles lay in readiness atop the little mounds of earth; a row of firing pits, a battle line. The bayonets, like sentinels, winked dully now and then, reflecting the light of distant fires along the front. Machine guns stood out starkly, tripods braced, muzzles peering ahead like eager, watchful dogs against the dark.
>
> The men were restful, wakeful, gathering about in little groups on blankets spread against the damp. They talked in quiet tones amongst themselves.
>
> Habit hid their cigarets against their breasts, still fearful that an enemy would spot the glow. Lone fellows took their ease in quiet, staring thoughtfulness. Why did they, like their bayonets, peer toward the front? Was something gone? Why did not a single one of them look toward the rear?
>
> There was a nervous tension in the air. It shattered when a fellow struck a match or laughed or raised his voice or moved too suddenly.
>
> At such time one saw men's heads snap up in quick alarm, in instant, wary watchfulness, and saw them search the shadows near at hand, then heard the hearty breath of quick relief as they remembered, trying to talk in a normal tone of voice, like normal men.
>
> Was there ever in the history of our race a night like that? So queer, so still, so full of listening?
>
> Silence laid a pall on everything that first night after the Armistice. The guns of four long years were still at last.

acclaim at Belleau Wood, overshadowing the army's great contribution to the war in Europe, a rivalry developed between the two services. Hard feelings spawned in the First World War were destined to carry over to the Second World War and would become instrumental in preventing the Marine Corps from fighting again in the European theater.

But petty rivalries cannot alter truth. When the last words are written about the bloody battle for Belleau Wood, the record will clearly show that it was the U.S. Marines who stood fast and stopped the Germans there.

Glossary

AEF: American Expeditionary Force; American armed forces in France during World War I.

air burst: an artillery shell equipped with a fuse and timed to explode above ground.

Allies: the Allied forces of France, Russia, Serbia, Great Britain, and Belgium in World War I; later joined by Italy, Rumania, Portugal, Montenegro, Japan, Australia, and the United States.

Balkans: the countries occupying the Balkan Peninsula, presently: Slovenia, Croatia, Bosnia, Herzegovina, Macedonia, Yugoslavia, Rumania, Bulgaria, Albania, Greece, and Turkey (in Europe).

bandolier: a closed loop of fabric with pockets for small-arms ammunition clips, usually worn by soldiers over the shoulder and across the chest.

barbed wire: a wire or strands of twisted wires with barbs or sharp points affixed; used to protect military defensive positions.

battalion: a body of troops made up of headquarters and two or more companies or batteries.

battery: a grouping of artillery pieces for tactical purposes.

bayonet: a steel blade attached to the muzzle of a rifle for use in hand-to-hand fighting; first used in Bayonne, France, in the seventeenth century.

Boche: a French slang term for a German or Germans; from the French word *Alboche*, a blend of *Allemand* (German) and *caboche* (head).

brigade: a military unit smaller than a division and larger than a regiment, with attached groups and/or battalions as needed to meet anticipated requirements.

Central Powers: the aligned powers of Germany and Austria-Hungary in World War I; later joined by Turkey and Bulgaria.

Chauchat: French 8mm automatic rifle.

contraband: goods or merchandise whose importation, exportation, or possession is forbidden.

corps: a tactical military unit usually consisting of two or more divisions and supporting arms and services.

Corps Conta: German corps named for and commanded by General Richard von Conta; principal units consisted of the 5th Guards Division and the 19th, 28th, 36th, 87th, 197th, 231st, and 237th Infantry Divisions.

Dépôt de la Guerre: French War Depot responsible for planning war operations.

Distinguished Service Cross: the U.S. Army's second-highest award for valor in action against an enemy.

division: a tactical combat unit or formation larger than a regiment or brigade but smaller than a corps.

firefight: a brief intense exchange of fire between infantry units.

foxhole: a small hole used for cover and to fight out of by one or two people.

gas mask: a mask worn over the face to filter gas from the air when the wearer inhales.

grenade: a small explosive or chemical missile of varied design. Grenades may be classified as hand or rifle grenades. More recent grenades are designed to be projected from special grenade launchers.

hachures: short lines used on a map for shading and denoting surfaces in relief and drawn in the direction of slope.

Heinie: the nickname for Heinrich and an American slang term for Germans in World War I.

H-Hour: the specific hour at which a military operation commences.

howitzer: a short artillery piece, larger than 30mm, used for firing shells at a high angle of elevation and low velocities.

Hun: a derogatory term for a German used during World Wars I and II; derived from the Asiatic warlike race of nomads who invaded and ravaged Europe during the fourth and fifth centuries.

Iron Cross: German medal awarded for bravery in action.

kamerad: German for comrade.

kilometer: five-eighths (.62) of a mile.

machine-gun nest: a machine-gun emplacement containing one or more machine guns.

Maxim: a recoil-operated, air-cooled, belt-fed heavy machine gun invented by American Hiram Maxim in 1883; an improved 1908 German version was used extensively by German soldiers in World War I.

Medal of Honor: the highest U.S. award for gallantry in action against an enemy.

minenwerfer: German trench mortar used to destroy machine-gun nests; literally, "mine thrower."

monkey meat: slang term for canned, boiled, Argentine corned beef.

mustard gas: a poison gas that burns the skin.

Navy Cross: the U.S. Navy's second-highest award for valor in action against an enemy.

no-man's-land: an unoccupied area between opposing trench lines.

155: a 1917 155mm gun of French design.

parapet: an elevation of earth or other material thrown up in front of a trench or emplacement to conceal or protect troops.

pavilion: a light building or other structure used as a shelter, as in a park; often used for dances or concerts.

PC: post of command.

platoon: a subdivision of a company-size military unit usually consisting of two or more squads or sections.

poilus: slang term for French soldiers; literally, "hairy ones."

quick-Dicks: Austrian 88mm light artillery.

regiment: a military unit larger than a battalion and smaller than a division.

section: a tactical unit of the U.S. Army and Marine Corps smaller than a platoon and larger than a squad.

75: U.S. 75mm field gun Model 1916.

skirmish line: a line of soldiers in advance of a battle line.

Springfield rifle: A .30-caliber bolt-action rifle used by U.S. troops, especially in World War I.

squad: a small party of soldiers grouped for tactical or other purposes.

status quo: the existing state of affairs.

strategy: the planning and directing of the entire operation of a war or campaign (*see also* tactics).

tactics: the art of placing or maneuvering forces skillfully in a battle (*see also* strategy).

Teufelhünden: German for "Devil Dogs"; German soldiers in World War I applied the name to the U.S. Marines.

trench: a ditch to protect soldiers from gunfire.

U-boat: German submarine; short for the German *unterseeboot*.

Vive les Marines!: French phrase for "Long live the Marines!"

whiz-bangs: German 77mm light artillery.

For Further Reading

Guy Chapman, *A Passionate Prodigality: Fragments of Autobiography.* New York: Holt, Rinehart and Winston, 1966. A major contribution to the literature of World War I, this book has been acclaimed as perhaps the finest nonfiction book to come out of the war; written by a British officer who served in the trenches with the Royal Fusiliers.

R. Ernest Dupuy and Trevor N. Dupuy, *The Encyclopedia of Military History.* New York: Harper & Row, Inc., 1977. A monumental work on warfare by two noted historians; includes a brief account of the Belleau Wood engagement and a comprehensive analysis of events occurring before and after that memorable battle in the woods.

George P. Hunt, *The Story of the U.S. Marines.* New York: Random House, 1951. An authentic history of the Marine Corps, from its beginning in 1775 through the Korean War, including a brief description of action at Belleau Wood; written by a decorated marine officer who served with the First Marine Division at Guadalcanal, Cape Gloucester, and Pelelieu during World War II.

Edward Jablonski, *A Pictorial History of the World War I Years.* Garden City, NY: Doubleday & Company, Inc., 1979. An overview of World War I, profusely illustrated with more than four hundred photographs and full-page maps.

John Keegan, *The Face of Battle.* New York: Viking Penguin, 1985. A classic study of battle by a former lecturer in military history at England's Royal Military Academy. The author's analysis of the First Battle of the Somme (July 1, 1916) portrays the horror of trench warfare during the greatest one-day loss of casualties in the history of the British army.

————, *A History of Warfare.* New York: Alfred A. Knopf, 1994. An examination of the world's major battlefields by one of the world's great military historians.

Erich Maria Remarque, *All Quiet on the Western Front.* New York: Little Brown, 1929. A primer on war in the trenches. This book has been claimed by countless reviewers as the greatest war novel of all time.

John Toland, *No Man's Land: 1918, The Last Year of the Great War.* New York: Ballantine Books, 1992. The story of one of the most fateful years in Western history, when the arrival of American troops in Europe turned a certain German victory into a decisive Allied victory. Historian John Toland writes history with all the drama and urgency of a suspense thriller.

Works Consulted

Robert B. Asprey, *At Belleau Wood*. New York: G. P. Putnam's Sons, 1965. A brilliant writer and unsurpassed historian, Asprey provides in this volume what will probably stand always as the defining book on the Battle of Belleau Wood. This book represents absolutely *must* reading for anyone who wants to learn about what happened there in the late spring of 1918.

John Ellis, *Eye-Deep in Hell: Trench Warfare in World War I*. New York: Pantheon Books, 1976. A detailed reconstruction of the soldier's daily life in the trenches, illustrated throughout with sketches and graphic photographs.

Floyd Gibbons, *"And They Thought We Wouldn't Fight."* New York: George H. Doran Company, 1918. The courageous war correspondent relates his experiences while covering the First World War for the *Chicago Tribune*. Gibbons was struck by three machine-gun bullets and lost his left eye while rushing to the aid of a wounded marine officer during the savage fighting for Belleau Wood.

Martin Gilbert, *The First World War: A Complete History*. New York: Henry Holt and Company, 1994. A dramatic narrative of the Great War that introduced tanks, planes, submarines, rapid-fire machine guns and artillery, and motorized cavalry to the arsenals of destruction; written by a contemporary historian of first rank.

James W. Hammond Jr., "Marines Take Belleau Wood," *Command Magazine*, September/October 1994. A fast-paced account of the marines in action in Belleau Wood; this article includes an excellent map and a collection of rare photographs of the battle area.

Marianne Hancock, "My Father Was a Hero," *U.S. Naval Institute Proceedings*, November 1978. A vivid account of a young marine second lieutenant's heroic actions and hand-to-hand fighting in Belleau Wood and beyond, told by his daughter sixty years later.

James G. Harbord, *The American Army in France*. Boston: Little, Brown, and Company, 1936. The memoirs of the U.S. Army general who commanded the 2d Division of the American Expeditionary Forces, of which the marine brigade formed a part during World War I. Harbord's remembrances include a personal account of the marines under his command at Belleau Wood.

Robert Leckie, *The Wars of America*. Vol. 2. New York: HarperPerennial, 1993. A compressed but comprehensive recounting of all of America's wars by a noted military historian who served in the Pacific with the Marine Corps in World War II. Volume 2 covers wars of the twentieth century, including World War I and the battle for Belleau Wood.

Elton E. Mackin, *Suddenly We Didn't Want to Die: Memoirs of a World War I Marine*. Novato, CA: Presidio Press, 1993. Mackin's memoirs offer a vision of war as can only be told by one who has viewed combat from the midst of it. Mackin, a much-decorated marine, captures both the horrors and the humdrum of life in the front lines, from Belleau Wood to the crossing of the Meuse in the final hours of the Great War.

S. L. A. Marshall, *World War I*. New York: American Heritage, 1985. A concise, clear one-volume history of the "war to end all wars," written by the dean of American military historians. Marshall sketches the Belleau Wood engagement in eight interesting pages.

Allan R. Millet, "Battle in Belleau Wood," *Naval*

History, Summer 1993. A brief account of the first week of fighting (June 3–10) for Belleau Wood.

J. Robert Moskin, *The Story of the United States Marine Corps*. New York & London: The Paddington Press, 1979. A history of the Marine Corps from 1775 through 1975; contains an excellent chapter of the marines in Belleau Wood.

James R. Nilo, "The Battle of Belleau Wood," *Leatherneck*, June 1993. A deft retelling of one of the Marine Corps' proudest hours, recalled seventy-five years after the encounter; illustrated with excellent photographs of battle terrain and those who fought there.

Ernst Otto, "The Battles for the Possession of Belleau Woods, 1918," *U.S. Naval Institute Proceedings,* November 1928. Otto offers an enemy's estimate of the marine as a soldier, in a detailed analysis of the Belleau Wood fighting; illustrated with rare photographs and hand-drawn maps.

Richard Suskind, *The Battle of Belleau Wood: The Marines Stand Fast*. Toronto: The Macmillan Company, 1969. The author captures the marines' rock-jawed determination to "stand fast" in Belleau Wood, with lightning prose, action photographs, and tactical maps.

John W. Thomason, *Fix Bayonets! and Other Stories*. New York: Charles Scribner's Sons, 1970. A collection of stories about the U.S. Marines in combat and on peacetime duty—from Belleau Wood to the Rhine, Peking (Beijing), the Gobi Desert, and the Banana Republics of Central America; written by a marine officer of twenty-seven years, who has been called "the Kipling of the Corps."

Index

Adams (American officer), 89-90

AEF (American Expeditionary Force), Pershing to command, 19-20

Allies, 9

The American Army in France (Harbord), 93

American Expeditionary Force (AEF), Pershing to command, 19-20

Baker, Newton D., 19

Barnett, George, 20-21

Battle of Belleau Wood
 capture of Hill 142, bloody and important, 50-58
 chronology of events, 8
 fight for Bouresches, 67-69
 foothold obtained, at cost, 59-69
 importance of, disagreement about, 48, 97, 101-102
 see also Belleau Wood; maps

The Battles for the Possession of Belleau Woods, June, 1918 (Otto), 94

Belfrey, Earl F., 68

Belleau Wood
 as Bois de la Brigade de Marine, 99
 description of terrain, 60

Berry, Benjamin S.
 action prior to Belleau Wood, 32, 34, 42, 50
 at Belleau Wood, 59, 61-62, 64-65, 73

Bismarck, Otto von, 10

Blanchfield, John, 33, 46, 80

Bliss, Tasker H., 101

blockades, 13-17

Boche (Germans), 27

Boehn, Max von, 34

Bois de la Brigade de Marine, Belleau Wood as, 99

Bouresches, fight for, 67-69

Britain
 blockades of and by, 13-15
 naval superiority, 15

Brown (American sergeant), 80-81

Brown, Preston, 44

Buford, David, 46

Bull Durham cigarettes, 34

Bundy, Omar, 23, 29, 32, 34, 42, 44, 48, 88

Cates, Clifton B., 68, 84-85, 100

Catlin, Albertus C.
 action prior to Belleau Wood, 37, 38, 49
 at Belleau Wood, 59-61, 66
 commands 6th Marine Regiment, 18-19, 21
 seriously wounded, 19

Central Powers, 9

Château-Thierry, German victory at, 27-28

Chicago Tribune, 62, 65

chronology of events, 8

City of Memphis (ship), 16

Cole, Edward B., 73

Colvin (American sergeant), 82

communications, always a problem, 38, 61, 74, 78, 80

Cooke, E. D., 32-33, 80-81, 82, 85

Corps Conta, 34, 40, 73

Crowther, Orlando C., at Hill 142, 50-51, 53, 56

Cummings, Sam, 76

Daly, Dan, 62

Degoutte, Jean M. J., 28, 34, 45, 48, 52, 86
 tribute to Marines, 99

Dockx, Francis J., 46

Doyen, Charles A., 20, 23, 29, 39

Duchêne, Denis A., 27, 35, 86

Dunbeck, Charles, 76-77, 80

Duncan, Donald F., 67

Eddy (American officer), 60

Erskine, Graves B., 67-68, 88

Europe, World War I map, 11

Evans, Francis, 69

Evans, Frank, 37

Feland, Logan, 79

Ferdinand, Francis (archduke of Austria-Hungary), 11-12

Finn (American corporal), 68

Foch, Ferdinand, 70, 97, 98

fog of war (confusion in battle), 77

food, a problem on both sides, 34, 91

foxholes, described, 33

France
 Franco-Prussian War, 9-10
 Second Republic, 10
 Third Republic, 10
 Franco-Prussian War (1870–1871), 9-10

Fuller, Benjamin H., 83

Fuller, Edward C., 82-83

gas. *See* mustard gas, use in WW I

George, Lloyd, 70

Germany
 1918 offensives
  Château-Thierry victory, 27-28
  Lys Offensive, 26, 42
  map, 29
  Somme Offensive, 26
 civilian starvations, 14
 soldiers earned Allies' respect, 43

Gibbons, Floyd, 62, 64, 65, 66

Grey, Sir Edward, 11

Hall (American private), 84

Hamilton, George W., at Hill

142, 50-51, 53-56

Harbord, James G.
  action prior to Belleau
    Wood, 32, 35, 47-48, 50
  army officer to command
    marines, 29
  at Belleau Wood, 59-60, 66,
    68, 71, 73-74, 78-80, 83,
    86-90, 96
  became honorary marine,
    87-88
  on German defensive
    position, 47-48
  on marines at Belleau Wood,
    99, 101
  on marines as heroes of
    June, 93
  on Pershing, 19-20
Hartzell, Oscar, 62, 64
Hebel (German private), 78
Hill 142
  assault, June 6, 1918, map,
    57
  bloody capture of, 50-58
Hindenberg, Paul von, 26
Hohenzollern (German
  dynastic family), 10
Holcomb, Thomas
  action prior to Belleau
    Wood, 29, 42
  at Belleau Wood, 67, 73,
    83-84, 88, 92, 96
Housatonic (ship), 16
House, Edward M., 10-11
Hughes, John A., at Belleau
  Wood, 73-74, 77, 80, 86, 92
Hunter, Daniel A., 54

Illinois (ship), 16
intelligence information,
  inaccurate and conflicting,
  48-49, 59-61,
    maps old and poor quality,
    55-56

Jackson (American
  lieutenant), 85
Janson, Ernest A., 57-58

Keyser, Ralph S., 92, 96
Kipling of the Corps, 51

Lay, Harry, 47
Lee, Harry, 66, 68-69
Le Gasse (American officer),
  47
Leitner, Aloysius, 81-82
Lloyd (American officer), 88
Ludendorff, Erich F. W., 26-27,
  42
Lusitania, sinking of, 13-14
Lys Offensive, 26, 42

Macklin, Elton E., 102
Maginot Line, 24
Malone, Paul, 32, 38
maps
  Belleau Wood
    marine attack, June 6, 69
    marine attacks, June 8–11,
      77
    marine attacks, June 12–15,
      86
    marine attacks (final),
      June 25–26, 92
  front line, June 4, 1918, 45
  German offensives, 1918, 29
  Hill 142 assault, June 6,
    1918, 57
  World War I in Europe, 11
maps, military, were old and
  poor, 55-56
marines
  action prior to Hill 142,
    32-39
  awarded Harbord honorary
    membership, 87-88
  baptism of fire in Europe,
    26-27
  joined AEF, without
    Pershing's blessings, 22-23
  lauded by Germans, 99
  training in Europe, 23-26
  win approval of Pershing, 27
  see also Belleau Wood; maps
Marshall, S. L. A., 31

Mathews, Bill, 74, 76
Maxim machine guns, 53, 55,
  61-62
Medal of Honor winners, 58,
  86
Meriweather, Lee, 75
minenwerfers (210mm trench
  mortars), 36, 41, 74
Moltke, Helmuth von, 10
monkey meat (corned beef),
  34
Moore, William B., 68, 93
mustard gas, use in WW I,
  26-27, 72, 82-86, 91, 93

Napoleon III (emperor of
  France), 10
Nash, Paul, 28
naval blockades, 13-17
Neville, Wendell C.
  action prior to Belleau
    Wood, 32, 58
  at Belleau Wood, 62, 79,
    87-88, 96
New York Times, 62, 70
Noble, Alfred H., 66
North German Confederation,
  10

Otto, Ernst, 52, 63, 94

Paris, in the springtime, 75
Pershing, John J., 29, 62, 79
  approves of marines'
    performance, 27
  did not request marines,
    22-23
  to command American
    Expeditionary Force (AEF),
    19-20
  on troops at Belleau Wood,
    97, 98, 101
Poe, Edgar (lieutenant), 82
Princip, Gavrilo, 12

quick-Dicks (88mm artillery),
  32
Quick, John H., 68, 93

Ridgway, Matthew B., 101
Robertson, James F., 67-68
Robinson (American officer), 47
Rockey, Keller, 53

Scott, Hugh, 20
Second Republic (France), 10
Shearer, Maurice
  action prior to Belleau Wood, 29, 32, 38, 43
  at Belleau Wood, 73, 83, 90, 92, 95-96
Shepherd, Lemuel C.
  on foxholes, 33
  on German infantry attacks, 36, 38
  on Wise, 25
Sheridan, Al, 67
Sibley, Berton W., 29
  at Belleau Wood, 59, 61, 66, 68, 70-71, 88, 92, 96
Smith, Dwight, 66
Somme Offensive, 26
Sophie (archduchess), 12
Stallings, Laurence, 90-92
starvation, by civilians, 14
Stockham, Fred W., 86
Suddenly We Didn't Want to Die (Macklin), 102
Swenson (American private), 67

Teufelhünden (Devil Dogs), 78
Third Republic (France), 10
Thomason, John W., Jr., at Hill 142, 52-54
  as Kipling of the Corps, 51

Timmerman, Louis T., 66-67, 73
Tismer (German officer), 52
Treaty of Frankfurt, 10
trenches, life in, 30
trench mortars, 36, 41, 74
Turrill, Julius S.
  action before Belleau Wood, 32, 34, 45, 50, 53, 56, 58
  at Belleau Wood, 83, 86, 88, 92

U-boats, 14-16
United States
  enters war with Allies, 16-17
  prior to WW I entry, 9-17
    breaks ties with Germany, 16
    declared neutrality, 13-16
Unterseebooten, 15

Villa, Pancho, 19
von Conta, Richard, 34, 40-42, 44
  tribute to marines, 99
von Diepenbroick-Grüter (German general), 34, 63
von Haxthausen (German general), 71, 73
von Jacobi (German general), 34
von Wilhelmi (German general), 34

Washington, John J., 19
Wass, Lester, 33, 80-82, 87
Western Front, 28, 30, 42
  front line, June 4, 1918, map, 45

whiz-bangs (77mm artillery), 32, 76, 83
Wilhelm II (kaiser of Germany), 9, 13, 26
Williams, Lloyd, 38, 39, 58, 76
Williams (American officer), 47
Wilson, Woodrow, 13-14, 16-17, 19, 101
Winans, Roswell, 86
Wise, Fredric M.
  action prior to Belleau Wood, 32, 34, 38-39
  at Belleau Wood
    early days, 58, 74
    final two weeks, 77-84, 86-88
  disagreement with Harbord, relieved, 92
  trained marines in France, 24-25
World War I
  chronology of events, 8
  German civilian starvations, 14
  life in the trenches, 30
  map, 11
  naval blockades, 13-15
  total deaths from, 12
  United States
    joins Allies, 16-17
    prior to entry, 9-16

Yowell, Robert, 96

Zane, Randolph T., 67-68
Zimmermann, Arthur, 14
  the Zimmerman telegram, 16

Picture Credits

About the Author

Earle Rice Jr. attended San Jose City College and Foothill College on the San Francisco peninsula after having served nine years with the U.S. Marine Corps.

He has authored thirteen other books for young adults, including adaptations of *Dracula* and *All Quiet on the Western Front.* Mr. Rice has written several books for Lucent, including *The Cuban Revolution, The Battle of Britain, The Inchon Invasion,* and *The Tet Offensive.* He has also written articles and short stories and worked for several years as a technical writer.

Mr. Rice is a former senior design engineer in the aerospace industry who now devotes full time to his writing. He lives in Julian, California, with his wife, daughter, granddaughter, three cats, and a dog.